# BRIGHT NOTES

# DAVID COPPERFIELD

# BY

# CHARLES

# DICKENS

## Intelligent Education

**IP** **INFLUENCE PUBLISHERS**

Nashville, Tennessee

BRIGHT NOTES: David Copperfield

www.BrightNotes.com

No part of this publication may be used or reproduced in any manner whatsoever without written permission, except in the case of brief quotations in critical articles and reviews. For permissions, contact Influence Publishers http://www.influencepublishers.com.

ISBN: 978-1-645420-52-1 (Paperback)
ISBN: 978-1-645420-53-8 (eBook)

Published in accordance with the U.S. Copyright Office Orphan Works and Mass Digitization report of the register of copyrights, June 2015.

Originally published by Monarch Press.
Paul M. Ochojski, 1964
2019 Edition published by Influence Publishers.

Interior design by Lapiz Digital Services. Cover Design by Thinkpen Designs.

Printed in the United States of America.

Library of Congress Cataloging-in-Publication Data forthcoming.
Names: Intelligent Education
Title: BRIGHT NOTES: David Copperfield
Subject: STU004000 STUDY AIDS / Book Notes

# CONTENTS

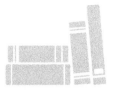

# INTRODUCTION TO CHARLES DICKENS

. . . . . . . . . . . . . . . . . . . . . . . . . . . . . . . . . . . . . . . . . . . . . . . . . . . . . . . . . . .

## EARLY LIFE

Charles Dickens was born on February 7, 1812, in Portsea. His father, John Dickens, was a minor clerk in the Navy Pay Office; his father's parents had been servants and his mother's parents only slightly higher on the social scale. John Dickens was a happy-go-lucky, improvident man whose family often knew want as the debts piled up. At the age of twelve, Charles Dickens experienced what was to become the key event of his life. His father was imprisoned for debt in the Marshalsea Prison; young Charles was taken out of school and put to work in a blacking warehouse in London, pasting labels on bottles of shoe polish. Although he later returned to school for a time, this experience left a permanent mark on the soul of Charles Dickens. Even many years later, after he had become a successful author, he could not bear to talk about it, or be reminded of his family's ignominy.

At the age of fifteen Dickens began working as an office boy for a law firm. He taught himself shorthand and by 1828 he became a reporter for the lay courts of *Doctors' Common*. The dull routine of the legal profession never interested him, so he became a newspaper reporter for the *Mirror of Parliament*, *The True Sun*, and finally for the *Morning Chronicle*. (John Forster, later his closest friend and biographer, was also employed at *The True Sun*.) By the age of twenty, Dickens was one of the best Parliamentary reporters in all England.

During this same period Dickens' interest began to switch from journalism to literature. His first work of fiction, "Dinner at Poplar Walk" (later reprinted as "Mr. Minns and His Cousin"), appeared in the *Monthly Magazine* when he was twenty-one. His newspaper work had given him an intimate knowledge of the streets and byways of London, and late in 1832 he began writing sketches and stories of London life. They began to appear in periodicals and newspapers in 1833, and in 1836 were gathered together as *Sketches by Boz, Illustrations of Every-day Life*, and *Every-day People*. This pseudonym, Boz, was suggested by his brother's pronunciation of "Moses" when he had a cold.

## PICKWICK PAPERS

The success of the *Sketches* brought an invitation from the publishers Chapman and Hall in 1836 to furnish the "letter-press" for a series of cartoon sketches about a humorous cockney sporting club. (The letter-press was little more than a running accompaniment, like an ornamental border around the drawings.) The project had hardly begun when Robert Seymour, the artist, committed suicide. Dickens searched long for a new artist and found an ideal collaborator in H. K. Browne ("Phiz"), but Dickens had persuaded the publisher to let him improvise a fictional narrative. When the *Posthumous Papers of the Pickwick Club* finally came out, the story predominated over the illustrations.

When *Pickwick Papers* appeared in April, 1836, as a monthly serial, the sales were at first discouraging. Of the first issue, a modest 400 copies were printed; later the work became increasingly popular. Some 40,000 copies of each issue were sold. After the last installment appeared in November, 1837, the novel was published in book form. This set the pattern for all of Dickens' subsequent novels.

The success of *Pickwick* convinced Dickens that his real career lay in writing fiction; he gave up his Parliamentary reporting in order to devote himself full time to it. In 1836 he had married Catherine Hogarth, the daughter of one of the owners of the *Morning Chronicle*; his growing family made it necessary to work exhaustingly at his writing. His next work, *Oliver Twist*, began appearing even before *Pickwick* was completed. Nicholas Nickleby followed in a like manner in 1838–39, and the very first number sold some 50,000 copies. During this same period he was editor of Bentley's *Miscellany* (1837–39). By the 1840s Dickens had become the most popular novelist in Britain, taking over the place long held by Sir Walter Scott.

## THE MIDDLE YEARS

The years between 1840 and 1855 were most fruitful ones: *The Old Curiosity Shop, Barnaby Rudge, A Christmas Carol, Martin Chuzzlewit, Dombey and Son, David Copperfield, Bleak House, Little Dorritt*, and *Hard Times* all appeared. In addition, he made his first trip to America; copyright laws at that time allowed American publishers to pirate his works, and their lack of concern over this injustice undoubtedly contributed to Dickens' unfavorable criticism of America in *Martin Chuzzlewit*. In 1850 Dickens founded his own periodical, *Household Words*, and continued to edit it until he and his partner exchanged it for *All the Year Round* in 1859. *Hard Times, A Tale of Two Cities*, and *Great Expectations* appeared in serial form in these publications.

But these years of literary success were marred by domestic strife. He and his wife had never been particularly suited to each other, and their marriage ended in separation in 1856.

In addition to writing, Dickens had another love - amateur theatricals - which led him into yet another pursuit in the latter part of his career. He gave public readings from his novels from 1859 to 1868 in England, Scotland, and America. He had always loved the theater - he studied drama as a young man and had organized an amateur theatrical company of his own in 1847 (he was both manager and principal actor).

His energies never seemed to fail: he burned the candle at both ends. He published *Our Mutual Friend* in 1864–65 and at his death left an unfinished novel, *The Mystery of Edwin Drood*, a suspense tale in the nature of a detective story. He died suddenly in 1870 from a stroke at the age of fifty-eight. G. K. Chesterton once said that Dickens died of "popularity." It would seem so; his exhaustive burden (marked by insomnia and fatigue) is well catalogued in his letters. He was buried in the Poets' Corner of Westminster Abbey.

Dickens wrote with an eye on the tastes of a wide readership, never far ahead of the printer, and was always ready to modify the story to suit his readers. For example, when the sales of serial installments of *Martin Chuzzlewit* fell from 60,000 to 20,000, Dickens sent his hero off to America in order to stimulate renewed interest. No novelist ever had so close a relationship with his public, a public ranging from barely literate factory girls to wealthy dowagers, but consisting mostly of the newly formed middle classes.

## TEACHER AND ENTERTAINER

Walter Allen in The English Novel points out that Dickens became the spokesman for this rising middle class, and also its teacher. "Dickens more than any of his contemporaries was the expression of the conscience-untutored, baffled, muddled as it doubtless often was-of his age," he writes. Not only in his novels, but in his magazine, Household Words, Dickens lashed out at what he considered the worst social abuses of his time: imprisonment for debt, the ferocious penal code, the unsanitary slums which bred criminals, child labor, the widespread mistreatment of children, the unsafe machinery in factories, and the hideous schools.

Yet, as Allen suggests, Dickens was primarily a great entertainer, "the greatest entertainer, probably, in the history of fiction." It is significant that Dickens was not satisfied to have his books the best sellers of their time. He wanted to see his audience, to manipulate it with the power of his own words. His public readings gave him an excellent opportunity to do so. Sitting alone on a bare stage, he would read excerpts from various novels, act them out really, imitating the voices of the various characters. These theatrical readings would always contain a dying-child scene or two which left his audience limp and tear-stained. Dickens suffered all the emotions with his audience, even after repeated readings, and this undoubtedly helped to shorten his life. He entertained his readers with humor, pathos, suspense, and melodrama, all on a grand scale. Charles Dickens had a fertile imagination that peopled his novels with characters and events which continue to entertain twentieth-century readers as they delighted his contemporaries.

## NOVEL TECHNIQUE

An understanding of Dickens as an artist requires an understanding of the method of publication he used-monthly or weekly installments. Serialization left its mark on his fiction and often accounts for the flaws which many critics have found in his work. John Butt and Kathleen Tillotson in *Dickens at Work* (1957) describe the problems serial publication imposed:

"Chapters must be balanced within a number in respect both of length and of effect. Each number must lead, if not to a **climax**, at least to a point of rest; and the rest between numbers is necessarily more extended than what the mere chapter divisions provide. The writer had also to bear in mind that his readers were constantly interrupted for prolonged periods, and that he must take this into account in his characterizations and, to some extent, in his plotting."

This technique brought on a loose, episodic treatment with a vast, intricate plot, numerous characters and much repetition to jog the reader's memory. Instead of the whole novel slowly building to a real **climax**, each part had to have a little **climax** of its own. In *Hard Times* the bad effects of serialization are at a minimum because it is a comparatively short novel (about 260 pages in most editions) and it appeared in weekly rather than monthly parts. But the careful reader can still tell where each part ended; considerations of space rather than of artistic technique formed the story.

The works of Dickens have many of their roots in the eighteenth century, especially in the novels of Tobias Smollett, whom he greatly admired. From Smollett he borrowed many devices of characterization - "tagging" characters with physical peculiarities, speech mannerisms, compulsive gestures, and eccentric names. Examples in *Hard Times* include the distinctive speech pattern of Stephen Blackpool, who talks in a phonetically transcribed Lancashire dialect; the self-deprecating speech of Bounderby or the self-pitying talk of Mrs. Sparsit; the physical peculiarities of Bitzer, the epitome of pallidness; the names of characters - Bounderby, M'Choakumchild, Gradgrind - so evocative of their personalities.

The eighteenth century also brought the picaresque tradition in fiction to full flower. (The term refers to novels which depict the life of a picaro [Spanish: "rogue"] and which consist of unconnected **episodes** held together by the presence of the central character.) Early novels, especially those of Defoe, Fielding, and Smollett, were rambling, episodic, and anecdotal. Many of the novels of Dickens-*Pickwick*, *Oliver Twist*, *David Copperfield* to name a few - are picaresque in technique. *Hard Times* borrows from the tradition only the irreverent, satirical view of stuffed-shirt pretentiousness and of established society in general. The eighteenth-century theater, with its sharply defined villains, its involved melodramatic plots, and its farcical humor, also suggested ideas for plots and characterizations to Dickens.

Dickens took his descriptive techniques from Sir Walter Scott and other early nineteenth-century novelists. No character, no matter how minor, appears on the scene without being fully described, not only as to physical appearance, but as to the clothing he wears. Dickens also excels in the short but evocative description of places; in *Hard Times* note the portrayal of the murky streets and factories of Coketown and of its blighted wasteland-like countryside.

## THE WORLD OF HIS NOVELS

The world of Dickens' novels is a fantasy world, a fairy-tale world, a nightmare world. It is a world seen as through the eyes of a child: the shadows are blacker, the fog denser, the houses higher, the midnight streets emptier and more terrifying than in reality. To a child, inanimate objects have lives of their own: thus the smoke malevolently winds over Coketown like serpents and the pistons of the steam engines in the factory are "melancholy mad elephants."

The characters, too, are seen as children see people. Their peculiarities are heightened to eccentricities; their vices, to monstrous proportions. Most of the people in his novels are caricatures, characterized by their externals, almost totally predictable in behavior. We know little about them beyond their surface behavior; Dickens focuses on the outward man, not the inner motives. It is interesting to note, however, that Dickens was able to create intensely individual portraits even though he lacked the ability to analyze motivation and character developments. His characters are more than types or mere abstract representations of virtue or vice. They are intensely alive and thus memorable. The characters from a Dickens novel are remembered long after the plots and even the titles of the books have been forgotten.

## DICKENS THE REFORMER

Dickens in his lifetime saw Great Britain change from a rural, agricultural "Merrie Old England" of inns, stagecoaches, and fox-hunting squires to an urbanized, commercial-industrial land of railroads, factories, slums, and a city proletariat. These changes are chronicled in his novels, and it is possible to read them as a social history of England. *Pickwick*, although set in 1827–28, reflects much of what still survived of the old eighteenth-century way of life. *Oliver Twist* (1837–39) shows the first impact of the Industrial Revolution - the poverty existing at that time and the feeble attempt to remedy it by workhouses. *Dombey and Son* (1846–48) describes the coming of the railroad, a symbol of change. Dombey, the merchant, sacrifices love, wife, and children for a position of power through money; yet he is already obsolete, for the industrialist is the ruler now.

Dickens grew increasingly bitter with each novel; his criticism of society became more radical, his **satire** more biting and less sweetened by humor. In his later novels he often broke out in indignant exasperation and almost hysterical anger. He figuratively mounted a soapbox, demanding that the "Lords and Gentlemen" do something about the appalling conditions of the poor.

In his early novels, society itself is not evil; it is only some people who are bad and who create misery for others by their callousness and neglect. By the time of *Dombey and Son* it is institutions which are evil, representing in that novel the self-expanding power of accumulated money. *Bleak House* (1852–53) attacks the law's delay and the self-perpetuating mass of futility it has become. *Hard Times* (1854) savagely lampoons the economic theories which Dickens considered responsible for much of human misery. The English historian, Lord Macaulay, charged that it was full of "sullen Socialism." Of *Little Dorritt* (1855–57), which attacks prisons and imprisonment for debt, George Bernard Shaw said that it was "more seditious than Karl Marx." In *Our Mutual Friend* (1864–65) we see the fully disillusioned Dickens. The atmosphere of the novel is grim, permeated with a sense of growing nightmare. There is the feeling that something deep and basic is wrong with the social order, something beyond the mere reforming of bad people or poorly-run institutions.

T. A. Jackson in *Charles Dickens: The Progress of a Radical* tries to claim him for the Marxists as a champion of the downtrodden masses. Yet Lenin, the father of Communist Russia, found Dickens intolerable in his "middle class sentimentality." George Orwell was probably correct when he stated that Dickens' criticism of society was neither political nor economic, but moral. Certainly Dickens offered no substitutes for the system or institutions he attacked. Thus in *A Tale of Two Cities* (1859) he expressed his loathing for the decadent French aristocracy of the ancient regime, but he seemed to like the triumphant democracy of the Revolution no better. In *Hard Times* he excoriates the exploitation of the industrial workers by the factory owners, but he is repelled almost equally by the attempt of the workers to form unions in self-defense. He seems to suggest that the Golden Rule is the only solution to class struggle.

# DAVID COPPERFIELD

## PREFACE

The justification for a book such as this is that it enables the average student to read with perception and understanding a work he might otherwise have found hopelessly perplexing and therefore distasteful. *David Copperfield* is a difficult work, although it has long been thought of as one of those novels in that literary limbo known as "Juvenile Classics." To a generation of students used to the straight-line progression of most television stories, the plot of *David Copperfield* seems incredibly intricate. Most of them find it difficult to remember the names and significance of scores of characters, while they try to follow several simultaneously developing sub-plots through the maze of leisurely-paced events.

This book can never be a substitute for *David Copperfield*, nor is it so intended. It is meant to introduce the student to a close reading of the work itself, to show him chapter by chapter as he reads the original, what Dickens is doing and why. Properly used, it will make the reading of *David Copperfield* a never-to-be-forgotten experience, because he will have been inside one of the world's greatest novels.

## SYNOPSIS OF THE NOVEL

David Copperfield was born at Blunderstone, six months after his father's death. Present at his birth was his aunt, Betsey Trotwood, an eccentric, strong-willed lady, who stalked out in a huff when informed that the baby was a boy, not a girl as she wished. David spent his early years with his mother, Clara Copperfield, a gentle but weak woman, and Peggotty, the combination servant and nurse.

When his mother marries again, to a Mr. Murdstone, David is sent off with Peggotty to Yarmouth to vacation with her family. Her brother, a fisherman, lives in a converted house-boat with his orphaned nephew Ham, his orphaned niece Little Em'ly, and the widow of his former partner, Mrs. Gummidge. David learns to love these simple people, and little Em'ly becomes his playmate.

On his return home, David soon discovers that his step-father and his sister, Miss Murdstone, who has moved in to run the household, are cruel tyrants. After biting Murdstone's hand during a savage beating, David is packed off to Salem House School near London. This institution is run by the ferocious Mr. Creakle, a sadist, but David makes two friends there, the lordly James Steerforth, and the somewhat dull but devoted Tommy Traddles.

After his mother and her newborn baby die, David is taken out of school by the Murdstones and put to work in a warehouse in London. There, half-starved, the 10-year-old David labors beside slum urchins. His only friend in this miserable life is Mr. Wilkins Micawber, a happy-go-lucky gentleman with whose family David boards.

When the Micawbers leave London to seek their fortune elsewhere, David, feeling completely friendless, runs away from the warehouse. He makes his way on foot to Dover where Aunt Betsey Trotwood, his only living relative, resides. He arrives there half-dead after having been bereft of all his possessions. His aunt takes him in and even repulses the Murdstones when they come to take him away. She sends him to Canterbury to attend a school, a good one run by Dr. Strong. He lives meantime in the home of Mr. Wickfield, Aunt Betsey's lawyer, and develops a brother-sister relationship with Agnes Wickfield, the sweet motherless daughter.

The time arrives when David, now 17, has completed his education and must seek a profession. He first meets Steerforth, now a college man, and renews their friendship. David has decided to become a lawyer and is articled to the firm of Spenlow and Jorkins in Doctors' Commons. On a visit to Yarmouth, David introduces Steerforth to Em'ly, now a pretty young girl engaged to Ham Peggotty. She is attracted to the lordly young gentleman.

On a visit to Agnes, David is warned against the evil influence of Steerforth. She also tells him that Uriah Heep, the Wickfield law clerk, is getting more and more power over her father, who has begun to drink heavily. Uriah tells David that he intends to marry Agnes someday.

In the meantime David has fallen in love with Dora Spenlow, the daughter of his employer. When he asks to marry her, Mr. Spenlow is furious, but soon after, he dies suddenly, leaving little money. A number of other tragedies come to pass about this time. Little Em'ly has run away with Steerforth, breaking the hearts of her uncle and Ham. Uriah Heep has gained full control of the Wickfield firm. Aunt Betsey has lost her fortune. David is now completely on his own.

He takes a part-time job with Dr. Strong, who is now retired in London. He learns shorthand in order to become a reporter. Traddles, his former school chum, encourages him in this and he succeeds. When he is 21, he marries Dora and begins a second career on the side, that of fiction writer. Although they are happy, Dora turns out to be an inept housewife and little help in his career. Soon after she gives birth to a baby who dies, she too fades away and dies. Coming after this tragedy is another; Steerforth is drowned in a gale off Yarmouth, and Ham dies trying to rescue him.

Micawber, who had become Uriah Heep's confidential clerk, reveals that Heep has been defrauding Mr. Wickfield for years (including Aunt Betsey's fortune) and unmasks him. Em'ly is reunited with her uncle after having been long searched for since her desertion by Steerforth. The Peggottys and Micawbers emigrate to Australia to begin a new life.

David spends three years on the Continent, trying to forget the tragedy in his life. He realizes also that he loves Agnes, the proper girl for him from the start, but he thinks it too late. He has in the meantime become a successful writer of fiction. At last he returns to England. When a little while later, he thinks that Agnes is about to marry, he blurts out his own love for her. He finds that she has loved him all along, and they are married.

The entire story is told by David as a grown man, a successful novelist, married to Agnes and now the father of several young children. He is reflecting on the events of his childhood and early career in a "memoir," which he says is for his eyes only.

# DAVID COPPERFIELD

## CHAPTERS 1–11

. . . . . . . . . . . . . . . . . . . . . . . . . . . . . . . . . . . . . . . . . . . . . . . . . . . . . . .

### CHAPTER 1: I AM BORN

David Copperfield was born at Blunderstone Rookery in the county of Suffolk. He never saw his father, who had died six months earlier and with whom he associates only the white gravestone in the churchyard, feeling an "indefinable compassion" for him "lying out alone there in the dark night."

On the day of David's birth, Miss Betsey Trotwood, his father's aunt, a lady of odd quirks and a strong will, made her first visit. David's father had been her favorite nephew, but when he had married the "wax doll" girl half his age who was to be David's mother, Miss Trotwood had become so angry that she never saw him again. The young widow is startled at the surprise visit of this fearsome lady, but she finds her kind, though gruff. Taking command of the household, Miss Trotwood orders Peggotty, the Copperfield servant girl, to make tea, and she decides that the baby will be a girl. "... I intend to be her friend," she states with authority, "I intend to be her godmother, and I beg you'll call her Betsey Trotwood Copperfield. There must be no trifling with her affections, poor dear. She must be well brought up, and well guarded from reposing any foolish confidences where they are not deserved. I must make that my care."

## Comment

Miss Trotwood's concern stems from her own unhappy marriage, she having long ago separated from a ne'er-do-well husband. She wishes to protect the child from the heartaches and disappointments of her own life. After Mrs. Copperfield tells Betsey that her husband has been good to her and has left her a small but adequate annuity, her labor pains begin. Peggotty sends her nephew, Ham Peggotty, for the nurse and the doctor, while Betsey stuffs cotton into her ears. Doctor Chillip, "the meekest of his sex, the mildest of little men," who "walked as softly as the Ghost in Hamlet, and more slowly," soon has to inform Miss Trotwood that the baby is a boy. After aiming a blow at the head of the meek Chillip with the bonnet she was holding, Miss Trotwood wordlessly "vanished like a discontented fairy," never to return.

## CHAPTER 2: I OBSERVE

David unfolds his reminiscences of his early childhood. He can recall his mother "with her pretty hair and youthful shape, and Peggotty, with no shape at all, and eyes so dark ..., and cheeks and arms so hard and red...." He remembers their house "... with a pigeon-house ... without any pigeons in it; a great dog-kennel in a corner, without any dog...." He remembers the parlors and the view of the churchyard from the bedroom window, thinks back to how he would romp with his mother and read to Peggotty from a book about crocodiles. Once he asked Peggotty if she had ever been married and if it were proper to marry again of one's spouse died. To the first question, Peggotty answers no, and the second one she evades.

## Comment

This foreshadows two events; the humorous courtship of Barkis, who is willing to marry Peggotty and eventually does, and the impending remarriage of David's mother, which is to destroy his idyllic childhood.

One day he meets a gentleman "with beautiful black hair and whiskers" who walks Mrs. Copperfield home from church. He takes an instant dislike to him, "jealous that his hand should touch my mother's...." Peggotty shares his aversion for Mr. Murdstone, for that is his name, and quarrels with her mistress over him, saying that "such a one as this, Mr. Copperfield wouldn't have liked." Mrs. Copperfield denies any romantic attachment to him and the whole household soon dissolves in tears of mutual recrimination.

## Comment

The name "Murdstone" is a good example of Dickens' technique of using names to symbolize people. "Murdstone" suggests both "murder (he was to bring David's mother to an early grave) and "stone" (his hardness of heart repels any attempt at affection by David).

One day Mr. Murdstone, now a regular visitor, takes little David on a horseback ride to nearby Lowestoft. In a hotel, he meets some of Murdstone's cronies, one of whom named Quinion makes some indiscreet remarks about the "pretty little widow." The naive boy of course does not know that Murdstone is after his mother's annuity.

Some months later David is sent away with Peggotty for a two weeks' visit with her brother in Yarmouth on the seacoast. He is joyful at the thought of boats and fishermen, and he recollects "how eager I was to leave my happy home, to think how little I suspected that I did leave forever." His last view is of Mr. Murdstone chiding his mother for her too-affectionate farewell.

## Comment

David and Peggotty have been sent away to allow Murdstone to marry Mrs. Copperfield and be able to spend an undisturbed honeymoon. The parting scene foreshadows the firmness which Murdstone will insist his new wife must share in their treatment of David.

## CHAPTER 3: I HAVE A CHANGE

After a long and roundabout ride in the carrier's wagon drawn by "the laziest horse in the world," David and Peggotty at last arrive at Yarmouth. David is at first disappointed by its appearance, for it "looked rather spongy and soppy, .... the town and the tide ... so much mixed up." But when he rides through the streets, smells the sea-odors and sees the sailors, he becomes delighted. Ham, Peggotty's nephew, now grown into a six-foot man, but "with a simpering boy's face," meets them. David is both amazed and pleased to find that the Peggotty home, a converted barge, is a real boat, now tidily furnished but still betraying its nautical origin. He is introduced to the Peggotty household. There is Mr. Daniel Peggotty, "a hairy man with a very good-natured face," a dealer in crabs and lobsters, and uncle to Ham, whose father had "drowndead." Little Em'ly, with those charms David is instantly smitten, is another orphan, the daughter of another "drowndead" brother. Mrs. Gummidge, the housekeeper, is the widow of Mr. Peggotty's former partner. Mr. Peggotty, a bachelor, supports them all, but is angered at the merest reference to his generosity. David falls asleep that first night listening to "the wind howling our at sea and coming across the flat."

## Comment

To the list of those drowned at sea will be added that of Ham, who will die in a howling storm off this very shore.

With this group of simple but good people, David spends a pleasant fortnight. He goes collecting seashells and pebbles with Little Em'ly, who tells him of her dreams of being a real lady, one of "gentlefolk," when she grows up. To show David that she does not fear the sea, she balances herself on a timber overhanging the water. David is frightened, but as he reflects on it now in maturity, he wonders if it had not been better had Emily fallen in then and perished.

## Comment

This frequent hinting at things to come is a characteristic technique with Dickens. This episodic creation of suspense was necessary in a story published in monthly serial installments.

When at last it is time for David to return home, he parts reluctantly from his little love, consoled only by the thought of seeing his beloved mother again. On the way, Peggotty breaks the news to him that he has "got a new pa." It turns out to be Mr. Murdstone, and his mother, instead of welcoming him with her usual affection, is told by her new husband. "Control yourself, always control yourself!" David creeps upstairs to bed, but finds that even the "old dear bedroom was changed, and I was to lie a long way off."

## CHAPTER 4: I FALL INTO DISGRACE

Peggotty and David's mother come upstairs to cheer up the troubled boy, but Mr. Murdstone, who follows them up, again urges "firmness." David realizes that Murdstone dominates his mother, "could mould her pliant nature into any form he chose." His stepfather privately warns David that he would beat an obstinate horse or dog into submission. "You understood me very well ...," he adds ominously. The mature Copperfield recollects that at this point one kind word of Murdstone's would have made their relationship different. "A word of encouragement and explanation, of pity for my childish ignorance, of welcome home, or reassurance to me that it was home, might have made me dutiful to him in my heart henceforth, instead of in my hypocritical outside, and might have made me respect instead of hate him."

## Comment

Dickens was among the pioneer crusaders for the rights of children. Here, as in other passages, he urges gentle understanding in place of the rigid, loveless discipline so prevalent in his day. His sympathy for unloved, abused, and exploited children grew into almost an obsession.

David's life is made even more miserable by the appearance of Miss Murdstone, his stepfather's sister, who has come to take over the housekeeping. He recollects that "when she paid the coachman she took her money out of a hard steel purse, and she kept the purse in a very jail of a bag which hung upon her arm by a heavy chain, and shut up like a bite." This "metallic lady" is also a great believer in "firmness" and David now comprehends "that it was another name for tyranny."

His mother at first resists the loss of authority, but is soon cowed into submission by the scowling pair. Gloom settles like a pall over the house. "The Murdstone religion ...was austere and wrathful" and Sunday becomes a day of dread for David, who is taken to church "like a guarded captive brought to a condemned service."

His education is similarly joyless. David recalls how easily he had learned to read by his mother's gentle tutoring, but learning now became "a grievous daily drudgery and misery." With Mr. Murdstone sitting by, he cannot learn at all, so intimidated is he. His only solace is in the world of books, a small library left behind by his dead father.

One day Mr. Murdstone appears for the daily lesson carrying a cane, which he swishes menacingly through the air. David, of course, does worse than usual, and although his mother mildly protests, he is taken upstairs to be caned. "He beat me then, as if he would have beaten me to death," he recalls. (David had bitten Mr. Murdstone's hand after the first blow.) Stopped finally by the crying of David's mother and Peggotty, his stepfather locks him into his room, where he remains for five days.

On the last night of imprisonment, Peggotty sneaks up and whispers through the keyhole that he is to be sent away to a school near London. She reassures him that she will look after his mother, and from that point on Peggotty takes a permanent place in David's heart. In the morning he takes leave of his mother, who has been persuaded that he is a bad boy, but whose maternal affection can be restraint only by the admonitions of the Murdstones.

## CHAPTER 5: I AM SENT AWAY FROM HOME

Before the cart taking David off to school has gone half a mile, it is overtaken by Peggotty. Saying not a single word, she hugs the boy, hands him a paper bag of cookies, and a purse. Then she disappears. David finds that the purse contains "two half-crowns folded together in a bit of paper, on which was written, in my mother's hand, 'For Davy. With my love.'"

In conversing with the cart driver, Mr. Barkis, a man "of a phlegmatic temperament, and not at all conversational," he finds that he is to be taken only as far as Yarmouth, there to transfer to the stagecoach for the London journey. Barkis tastes some of the cookies, finds that they were made by Peggotty, ascertains that she has no sweethearts, and then tells David that when he writes to her he is to relay the message, "Barkis is willin'."

When he arrives at the Yarmouth inn, David finds that a paid-for dinner awaits him It is served by a friendly waiter who frightens him with stories of the disasters befalling the gluttonous, and who "helps" him eat the largest share of the dinner.

## Comment

This account of the naive David being cheated out of most of his dinner by the cunning waiter is a prime example of Dickens as a comic writer.

Soon he mounts the London stage and after an unpleasant trip, hungry and cramped, he is dropped off at his destination, an inn in the Whitechapel district. Here his sense of fearful apprehension is increased, for there is no one to meet him David has fears of slowly starving to death amid the uncalled-for luggage when his few coins are used up. He therefore feels relieved when "a gaunt, sallow young man with hollow cheeks" asks for him. It is Mr. Mell, one of the masters at Salem House (the boarding school), an awesome personage in little David's eyes. They make their way through the turmoil of London to an almshouse where an old woman prepares breakfast for David. It is Mell's mother, living this way because of his meager salary. While David eats, Mell performs horribly on the flute at his mother's request.

Soon they continue on to the school, where they are greeted by "a stout man with a bull neck, a wooden leg, over-hanging temples, and his hair cut close all around his head." No pupils are there, for it is the holiday season and David had been sent early as punishment. He is forced to wear a sign, "Take care of him. He bites." Lonely and harassed, David recollects, "I positively began to have a dread of myself, as a kind of wild boy who did bite." He dreads the soon-approaching day when his fellow pupils will return, and he wonders how they will take to him.

## CHAPTER 6: I ENLARGE MY CIRCLE OF ACQUAINTANCE

Several dreary weeks go by before Salem House school reopens and David is taken to meet the returned headmaster, the ferocious Mr. Creakle. A stout gentleman with fiery face, small deep-set eyes, a thin nose and thick veins on his forehead, Mr. Creakle speaks only in whispers, the wooden-legged man repeating his statements for him. It turns out that he knows Mr. Murdstone and has been instructed that David's "teeth are to be filed."

David also makes the acquaintance of his fellow pupils, one of whom, Traddles, instantly befriends him. He is introduced also to J. Steerforth, an older boy who is a privileged pupil because of his family's wealth. Steerforth, good-looking, self-assured and rather condescending in his manner, appropriates David's few shillings to give a party. He promises "to take care of" David, and the grateful boy is happy to have found so imposing a protector.

From the boys he finds out that Mr. Creakle and his wooden-legged voice, Tungay, had been hop dealers "who had taken to the schooling business after being bankrupt in hops." Creakle, a sadist whose chief delight is in beating the boys, especially the smaller ones, is "more ignorant than the lowest boy in school." He had turned away his own son for protesting his cruelty. Only Steerforth is exempt from his beatings.

## Comment

This acidly-etched picture of a boys' school is only one of a number of such in the novels of Dickens. In Nicholas Nickleby, an earlier novel, Dickens vented the full force of his fury on the dismally meager education and the body-and-soul-warping cruelty found in these schools. His attacks resulted in a Parliamentary investigation and a closing of the worst of them.

## CHAPTER 7: MY 'FIRST HALF' AT SALEM HOUSE

The next day, school begins in earnest. Mr. Creakle, through his henchman Tungay, admonishes the assembled pupils, "Take care of what you're about, in this new half. Come fresh up to the lessons, I advise you, for I come fresh up to the punishment. I won't flinch." To David, with blows of his cane to punctuate his remarks, he says that if David is famous for his biting, so is his cane. In the course of the day most of the boys feel the bite of his cane for various infractions, real or imaginary. David recollects that "there never can have been a man who enjoyed his profession more than Mr. Creakle did. He had a delight in cutting at the boys, which was like the satisfaction of a craving appetite."

## Comment

Although Dickens lived before Freud, he often demonstrates shrewd psychological insights. He is here delineating the classic type of sadist, the pervert who derives satisfaction by the infliction of cruelty. In the time of Dickens, sadists often found outlets for their passions by serving as schoolmasters. They often escaped notice because flogging was so common a practice.

Traddles, his friend, is often the victim of Creakle's cane, sometimes taking the punishment meant for others, once for Steerforth. Steerforth, who is worshipped by David, keeps on "taking care" of him, helping him with his lessons in return for

David's entertaining him by nightly recitations of the contents of the novels he has read. David reflects that "whatever I had within me that was romantic and dreamy, was encouraged by so much story-telling in the dark...." And so life went on month after dreary month. "In a school carried on by sheer cruelty ... there is not likely to be much learnt." Yet David managed to "pick up some crumbs of knowledge."

Two events broke the deadly monotony. One day Mr. Mell, for whom David had retained his early liking, engaged in an exchange of words with Steerforth, who had always treated him with contempt for his obvious poverty. Called "an impudent beggar" for daring to admonish Steerforth, Mr. Mell reports him to Creakle. But Creakle, deferring to his prize pupil, summarily dismisses the unfortunate master when informed by Steerforth that Mell's mother lives in an almshouse. Traddles is caned for sympathizing with Mr. Mell. David is torn between sympathy for Mell and his admiration for Steerforth; the latter wins out.

The second event is the unexpected visit of Mr. Peggotty and Ham. David is overjoyed to see his old friends and hear news of Little Em'ly, who, he hears, is getting to be a woman. Steerforth, who happens by, is introduced to the pair and makes an instant hit with them with his magnetic personality. He is invited to visit the Peggottys any time he is in Yarmouth. David wonders whether he should tell Steerforth about Em'ly, but decides not to.

The half year draws to a close with "dog's-eared lesson-book, cracked slates, tear-blotted copy-books, canings... and a dirty atmosphere of ink surrounding all." The time at last comes in which David is to go home for a holiday.

## Comment

In this chapter the groundwork has been laid for two future events. David's story-telling is the seed of his later career as a story writer. Steerforth has met the Peggotty's, into whose lives he will bring tragedy as the seducer of Little Em'ly and the cause of Ham's death. His character is revealed on several occasions, although the hero-worshipping David does not recognize it. Steerforth is arrogant, selfish, callous to the feelings and sufferings of others.

## CHAPTER 8: MY HOLIDAYS. ESPECIALLY ONE HAPPY AFTERNOON

After a dreary trip on the Yarmouth stagecoach and a sound sleep at the inn, David finds himself called for again by Mr. Barkis, the taciturn cart-driver who is to take him the rest of the journey. "He received me exactly as if not five minutes had elapsed since we were last together…," the mature David muses in retrospect. Barkis tells David that he has received no answer to his message to Peggotty that he is willin', and he asks that the message be repeated.

David arrives at his home, finds it little changed in appearance except that his mother "was suckling an infant, whose tiny hand she held against her neck." As the Murdstones are away on a visit, David has a few happy hours with his mother and his new little brother. Thinking now about the reunion, he writes, "I wish I had died. I wish I had died then, with that feeling in my heart. I should have been more fit for heaven than I ever have been since."

David tells Peggotty of Barkis' message, but she laughs and says she wouldn't marry him "if he was made of gold." She wants only to take care of her mistress and to protect her from the wiles of the Murdstones. That night the Murdstones return and David's brief happiness is at an end. Miss Murdstone is obvious in her dislike for him, checking the holidays off on a calendar as if that would hasten his return to school. David sulks in his room or sometimes sits in the kitchen with Peggotty. Both things he is forbidden to do by Mr. Murdstone, who accuses him of being disrespectful by avoiding them or preferring "the low company" of the servants. David spends the remainder of the vacation in misery, sitting stupidly and stiffly in the parlor with them night after night.

Soon the day of his departure comes. Barkis appears with his cart to fetch him and David kisses his mother and baby brother goodbye, "not sorry to go away, for the gulf between us was there." He was never to see his mother alive again.

## Comment

Dickens in this chapter shows off his ability at pathos, the sentimental heart-wringing so loved by his Victorian audience. There are a number of hints of the impending death of David's mother which the reader gets, but which little David at the time does not surmise. We can thus feel sorry for him in advance.

## CHAPTER 9: I HAVE A MEMORABLE BIRTHDAY

When David's tenth birthday arrives, he is still a pupil at Salem House. "How well I recollect the kind of day it was! I smell the fog that hung about the place...I look along the dim perspective of the schoolroom, with a sputtering candle here and there to light up the foggy morning…," he writes. He expects a hamper of presents from Peggotty and therefore hurries to Mr. Creakle's office when summoned. Mrs. Creakle leads him to a sofa and gently breaks the news to him. His mother is dead.

David is inconsolable, feeling himself now completely "an orphan in the wide world." Among his school fellows he enjoys briefly a feeling of importance which eases his grief. The next night he is hurried home for the funeral. He is not met by Barkis this time but by a "merry-looking, little old man in black," Mr. Omer, the local undertaker, haberdasher, tailor and draper. He is taken into the shop, measured for a suit of mourning, and there meets Minnie Omer, the undertaker's pretty young daughter, and Joram, Omer's assistant and her sweetheart. During the ride to his house, he is puzzled that they should be so cheerful while he is so sad.

At home Peggotty comforts him, but Mr. Murdstone takes no heed of him and Miss Murdstone is concerned only with taking inventory of everything, including David's clothes. The day of the funeral arrives, and amid his sobs he sees "that good and faithful servant, whom of all people upon earth I love the best," Peggotty. She is all that now links him to his once happy childhood.

That night, after they return home, Peggotty comes to his room and tells him of his mother's final days. She had faded little by little in the loveless and oppressive atmosphere of the Murdstones. At last she had "died like a child that had gone to sleep" and the little baby had died soon after. David reflects, "The mother who lay in the grave, was the mother of my infancy; the little creature in her arms, was myself, as I had once been, hushed forever on her bosom."

## Comment

In the narration of the decline and death of David's mother, Dickens pulls out all the stops. The pathos of the previous chapter descends into the bathetic (tear-jerking we would call it today). But it is exactly these scenes that the Victorians found most enjoyable, and Dickens was often requested to read these at recitals.

## CHAPTER 10: I BECOME NEGLECTED, AND AM PROVIDED FOR

Immediately after the funeral, Miss Murdstone fires Peggotty, giving her a month's notice. David feels that, if possible, he would have been dismissed with a month's notice too. But nothing happens, except that he is strangely left to his own devices. The former restraint is gone and the Murdstones just ignore him. He feels abandoned and has fears of "growing up to be a shabby, moody man, lounging an idle life away...."

When Peggotty, who is unable to find employment in the neighborhood, returns to her kinfolk in Yarmouth, David is oddly permitted to go with her. Barkis comes to take them there and on the ride carries on his peculiar courtship of Peggotty. On their arrival, Peggotty asks David whether she should marry Barkis and he gives his opinion that it would be a good thing.

At the Peggottys' barge house, everything is the same except that Little Em'ly if off at school. However, soon she comes home and David is pleased at how she has grown into a pretty young miss. They talk of Steerforth, whom David praises to the skies, and Em'ly seems infected with David's admiration for his school friend. One day they all go on a picnic in the cart of Barkis. Peggotty and Barkis stop off at a church and on their return David finds that they have been married. He feels abandoned again when Peggotty joins her new husband in his house, but is consoled by the thought of staying with Little Em'ly, whom he firmly expects to marry someday.

The happy holiday is soon over and David returns to his own sorrowful home. The Murdstones continue their neglect and he falls "into a solitary condition - apart from all friendly notice ... apart from all companionship" but his "own spiritless thoughts." This he finds worse than being ill-used, beaten or starved. Only Dr. Chillip, the old family physician who had brought him into the world, occasionally invites him over, and Peggotty visits him once a week, bringing little gifts.

## Comment

Over and over again, Dickens throughout this novel, as in almost every other, dwells as in this scene on the callous, loveless neglect of children which is worse than physical abuse, because its long-range effects are greater.

One day Mr. Quinion, Murdstone's friend, reappears and it is he who suggests the scheme that will forever determine David's later life. He is not to return to school. "Education is costly," says Mr. Murdstone, "... and I am of the opinion that it would not be at all advantageous to you to be kept at school." He is to go instead to London, to the firm of Murdstone and Grinby, there to be employed for his room and board. David understands that the Murdstones want to get rid of him, but recalls neither pleasure nor fright at the prospect.

## CHAPTER 11: I BEGIN LIFE ON MY OWN ACCOUNT, AND DON'T LIKE IT

Even now, the adult David Copperfield cannot understand how he could "have been so easily thrown away at such an age" without anyone to make a sign in his behalf. But no one lifted a finger to help him and so he became at the age of ten a little laborer in the service of Murdstone and Grinby. The warehouse turns out to be "a crazy old house with a wharf of its own, abutting on the water, ... overrun with rats ... its panelled rooms, discoloured with the dirt and smoke of a hundred years...." Here he is put to work, along with several other boys, at washing empty bottles, pasting on labels, and packing cases. "No words can express the secret agony of my soul as I sunk into this companionship," he remembers. "... and I felt my hopes of growing up to be a learned and distinguished man crushed in my bosom."

## Comment

Here Dickens is revealing, slightly disguised, an autobiographical event, so painful to him in memory that he could not bear to speak of it in later life. He too had been taken out of school and put to work in a factory (pasting labels on bottles of blacking), and the sufferings of David must have been his too. David was an orphan; Dickens was not, and this made it worse. He never forgave his parents.

David is introduced to Mr. Micawber, with whose family he is to board, according to Mr. Murdstone's arrangements. Mr. Micawber is "a stoutish, middle-aged person ... with no more hair upon his head ... than there is upon an egg." He wears shabby clothes, but sports a tasseled cane and a quizzing-glass (a sort of monocle). His manner of speaking is flowery and roundabout, but David takes a liking to him. David is taken to his new lodgings, a shabby but pretentious house where he is presented to Mrs. Micawber, "a thin and faded lady, not at all young ..." with a baby (one of twins) always at her breast. The rest of the household consists of two other children and the "Orfling," the poor-house orphan who is the maid-of-all-work.

It is not long before David becomes intimate with the Micawbers and is familiar with their pretentions and problems: Mrs. Micawber's pretensions of a genteel family background, and Mr. Micawber's problems of keeping ahead of his numerous creditors. In spite of their troubles, the Micawbers seem to lead a happy-go-lucky life. David's life is not so pleasant. The work at the warehouse is deadening, his fellow workers are "common men and boys," and he "lounged about the street, insufficiently and unsatisfactorily fed."

He becomes an efficient worker and is learning about life the hard way. He learns how to take articles to the pawn shop, which he often does for the Micawbers. At last Mr. Micawber can stave off his creditors no longer and he is imprisoned for debt in the King's Bench Prison. David visits him there, and later when Mrs. Micawber had moved into jail, too, he often breakfasts with them. They seem better off in prison, David observes.

## Comment

Dickens is again giving us a glimpse into a secret compartment of his own life. He too as a boy used to visit his father in debtor's prison, the Marshalsea, In fact, the whole **episode** of the Micawber's insolvency, the spoon-and-book pawning, the gradual emptying of the house as the furniture was sold off, the living in jail, are all like the actual boyhood experience of Dickens, as he himself told Forster, his friend and biographer.

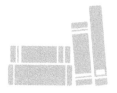

# DAVID COPPERFIELD

## CHAPTERS 12–21

. . . . . . . . . . . . . . . . . . . . . . . . . . . . . . . . . . . . . . . . . . . . . . . . . .

### CHAPTER 12: LIKING LIFE ON MY OWN ACCOUNT NO BETTER, I FORM A GREAT RESOLUTION

At last a settlement is made with Micawber's creditors and that gentleman and his family are released from prison. David helps them celebrate, but is downcast when told that they will move to the country, where Mrs. Micawber's family will help them out "until something turns up." Realizing that he is gain to be left friendless and alone, that night he walks home to make a decisive resolve. When he bids farewell to the Micawbers as they mount the stagecoach, he determines to run away to seek out his great-aunt Betsey Trotwood. He remembers his mother's stories of her singular visit at his birth and he has the feeling that this awesome personage would be kindly disposed towards him.

He finishes out his week at the warehouse and with a half-guinea coin borrowed by mail from Peggotty, he sets out on foot for Dover. His box, containing all his possessions, is stolen by a young man who is to take it to the shipping office, along with the half guinea. Poor David, exhausted with the futile chase of the thief and left with nothing but the clothes he is wearing and a few small coins, at last sets out on his journey.

## CHAPTER 13: THE SEQUEL OF MY RESOLUTION

After walking awhile and having dire thoughts of being found starved to death beneath some hedge, David remembers his pawn-shop trips for the Micawbers. He sees a second-hand clothes shop and there he sells his waistcoat (vest) for ninepence, a small price, but one the inexperienced boy is happy to get. He will at least have some money for food on the long trip to his aunt's house in Dover.

The next evening finds him in the vicinity of Salem House, his old school. He finds a haystack in a corner of the wall and lies down in sight of its darkened windows. "Never shall I forget the lonely sensation of first lying down, without a roof over my head," he recalls. Early the next morning, a Sunday, he sets out again and that day covers twenty-three footstore miles. On Monday, dusty and with tangled hair, he enters Chatham looking for a shop to sell his jacket. He finds a dingy den run by "a dreadful old man ... in a filthy flannel waistcoat, and smelling terribly of rum." The old man, "there never was such another drunken madman in that line of business," makes him lose the better part of the day waiting for his money, trying to make him take all sorts of useless things in exchange. On the road he is frightened by tramps and has his silk neckerchief stolen from him by a rough young tinker.

After six days of wandering, with ragged shoes, dust-covered, sunburned, and half-clothed, he arrives in Dover. He has some difficulty locating his aunt's house, but finally stands before it, "a very neat little cottage with cheerful bow-windows." Hesitatingly, he approaches the lady who comes out, dressed for gardening. It is his aunt, and in a minute he blurts out his pitiful story and breaks down into a fit of crying. Mr. Dick, the kindly but eccentric old gentleman who boards with Betsey Trotwood, is asked what should be done with David. "Wash him," is his unexpected but practical suggestion. While is bathed and fed, his aunt and her servant girl Janet occasionally rush outside to drive away donkeys which are ridden so as to trespass on her front yard. This was "the one outrage of her life, demanding to be constantly avenged ..."

After a nap and a good dinner, the first in weeks, David tells his aunt about his mother's marriage to Murdstone and of his life since. He is shown to bed in a pleasant room and falls asleep praying that the "never might be houseless any more, and never might forget the houseless."

## Comment

This chapter is an excellent cross-section of the Dickens style at its best. It has suspense, humor, action, and pathos. In it Dickens portrays one of the grotesques he loved to depict, the mad old-clothes dealer in Chatham. Again and Again Dickens tugs at the heart-strings and we are as relieved as David when he reaches at last that snug and comfortable bed.

## CHAPTER 14: MY AUNT MAKES UP HER MIND ABOUT ME

David comes down to breakfast to find his aunt absent-minded in deep sales thought and he is sure that he is the subject of it.

He wonders what she will decide to do about him. He is then told that she has written Mr. Murdstone of his whereabouts and that a decision will be made after a meeting. Until that fateful day arrives, David makes the better acquaintance of Mr. Dick, his aunt's companion. Richard Babley, for that was his real name, is a harmless lunatic whose brother wanted him committed to an asylum but whom Betsey Trotwood had taken in instead. His chief occupation consists in writing a long memorial to the Lord Chancellor and flying a huge kite upon which the memorial is to be "taken far away." Mr. Dick is perturbed because the head of King Charles I keeps being mentioned in the memorial; he can't seem to keep it out.

## Comment

In this **episode** of Miss Trotwood and the harmless lunatic, Mr. Dick, Dickens is suggesting a remedy for the unenlightened if not harsh treatment of the insane in his time. He suggests that many of them (as we now know) would benefit by kind treatment in a home-like atmosphere.

When the Murdstones arrive, it is not under the best circumstances. They ride their donkeys rough-shod over Betsey Trotwood's front yard and are immediately repulsed. The confrontation of the irascible Betsey and the venomous Miss Murdstone is especially hostile. A truce is declared and the Murdstones enter the house to deliberate David's fate.

Miss Betsey is informed that David has "a sullen, rebellious spirit, a violent temper, and an untoward, intractable disposition." Miss Murdstone adds that he is the worst boy in the whole world. The negotiations soon break down into violent disputations. Mr. Murdstone declares that if Betsey insists on abetting David, he will wash his hands of him. Betsey in turn accuses Murdstone of having caused his wife's death and of not wanting David around as a constant reminder. She declares that she will accept the responsibility for David and that if the Murdstones will trespass on her yard again she will knock Miss Murdstone's bonnet off. The crestfallen Murdstones beat at a hasty retreat.

Miss Betsey announces to David that she and Mr. Dick are now jointly his guardians and that he is henceforth to be called Trotwood Copperfield. "And thus I began my new life, in a new name, and with everything new about me." muses Copperfield as he writes his story.

## Comment

Mr. Dick and Betsey Trotwood are the second set of substitute parents for David. In Mr. and Mrs. Micawber, his first, Dickens had depicted a little of his own parents, his improvident father and ineffective mother. As Edgar Johnson points out in Dickens; His Tragedy and Triumph, Betsey Trotwood is the fairy godmother who disperses the evil Murdstones with a wave of the magic wand, and shuts out the warehouse forever. She is what every orphaned or neglected child should have, but has only in dreams.

## CHAPTER 15: I MAKE ANOTHER BEGINNING

David and Mr. Dick become the best of friends. Often, after Mr. Dick had labored long on another of his memorials which came to nothing because the head of King Charles kept creeping in somehow, they would go out to a hillside and fly the huge kite. It was then that Mr. Dick was happiest. One day, David, whose new name had been by now affectionately shortened to Trot, is told by his aunt that he is to go to school in nearby Canterbury.

The next day they ride off in a rented pony cart, stopping off at Mr. Wickfield's house, her lawyer's, to inquire about the school. At the door of the quaint old-fashioned house they are greeted by the law-clerk, Uriah Heep. He is a 15-year-old youth with close-cropped red hair, a cadaverous face, red-brown eyes and long skeleton hands. As Aunt Betsey and Mr. Wickfield talk about him, David sees Uriah Heep stealthily staring at him with him sleepless eyes ... like two red suns."

## Comment

Here we are in the presence of another villain, Uriah, Heep, whose very name suggests his crawling (creep) nature. It is Uriah who ruins Aunt Betsey financially, causes near-tragedy for the Wickfields and Micawbers. How he is foiled is one of the plot threads of the later chapters.

Aunt Betsey is not satisfied with any of the boarding houses at which David could stay (he cannot board at the school). A solution is found by which David is to board with the Wickfields. Mr. Wickfield takes them to meet his "little housekeeper," his daughter Agnes. David sees a girl about his own age with a sweet, placid face which seems always surrounded by light. His aunt leaves to return home, giving David some parting advice, "Never be mean in anything; never be false, never be cruel." That first evening in his new home, David watches Agnes as she entertains her father, but he notices that the old gentlemen drinks too much port wine. Before he goes to bed he has occasion to shake Uriah's hand, but so ghostly-clammy is its touch that he feels the need "to rub his off."

## Comment

David, unaware, has met his future second wife, Uriah Heep, who secretly aspires to her, is to become his bitter enemy.

## CHAPTER 16: I AM A NEW BOY IN MORE SENSES THAN ONE

The next morning David is taken to the Canterbury school and there he meets Dr. Strong, the head master. He is a man in "clothes not particularly well-brushed," untidy, absent-minded, and much older than his pretty wife, Annie, whom David mistakes at first for his daughter. David later learns that he had married her for love only a year before and that now he is saddled with a host of poor in-laws. There is his mother-in-law, Mrs. Markleham, called "the Old Soldier" by the schoolboys, who lives with them. There is also a cousin, Jack Maldon, once Annie's childhood sweetheart, who is to be provided for by being sent to India to make his fortune.

While David is learning about this new establishment, he is attending Dr. Strong's classes. At first he feels strange among the boys, ashamed of his sordid life in the London warehouse, and afraid one of the boys will recognize him as the ragged urchin who walked through Canterbury only a short time ago. But "in a very little while, the Murdstone and Grinby life became so strange to me that I hardly believed in it ...," he writes.

"Doctor Strong's was an excellent school; as different from Mr. Creakle's as good is from evil." The honor and faith of the boys were appealed to, rather than their fear of the cane. The pupils felt they had a share in the school and "learnt with a will, desiring to do it credit." "We had noble games out of hours, and plenty of liberty." The Doctor himself was the idol of all the pupils, a kind man with a simple faith which often made him the dupe of sharpers.

## Comment

Dickens had decided views on education and was highly critical of the repressive measures then in vogue in most schools. Here he is describing the ideal school, just as in Creakle's he is describing the worst type.

At home with the Wickfields, David gets to know Uriah Heep better. Heep spends most of his spare time studying law, but protests that he is to 'umble to think of becoming Mr. Wickfield's partner someday. He slyly keeps prying into David's relationship with his master, insinuating that David is to be the law partner someday. This makes David uneasy, as he has no such intentions. Toward Agnes he develops an increasing affection, but, as he says, "I love little Em'ly, and I don't love Agnes-no, not at all in that way - but I feel that there are goodness, peace, and truth wherever Agnes is."

## Comment

In this chapter the foundations are laid for two future developments. One is the subplot involving Dr. Strong and his wife. (Dickens was fond of weaving in secondary or subplots the minor characters. The Peggotty-Barkis romance is one such device, the Micawbers' affairs another.) The other development foreshadowed faintly is the eventual romance between David and Agnes, whom he marries after the death of his first wife.

## CHAPTER 17: SOMEBODY TURNS UP

The weeks pass quietly at Dr. Strong's school. David hears from Peggotty that his old home is now empty and up for sale, the Murdstones having gone. She is happy as Mrs. Barkis although she finds him a bit stingy.

David's great-aunt at first comes to see him frequently and at unexpected times, with the view of taking him by surprise, he thinks. But as she finds him doing well in school, her inspection trips cease, and instead David goes to visit her from time to time. Mr. Dick, her addle-headed companion, comes to see him every other Wednesday. He tells David of a mysterious beggar who hangs about Miss Betsey's house, a man whose first appearance caused her to faint and to whom she secretly gives money. David thinks this story a figment of Mr. Dick's fantastic imagination.

## Comment

Dickens is again creating a new line of suspense, so necessary for his serialized novel. The mysterious stranger turns out to be Aunt Betsey's long lost husband, but not until Chapter 47, and after he has reappeared several other times under strange circumstances.

Mr. Dick, so child-like himself, is very popular with David's fellow pupils, taking an interest in their games and being very handy in making unusual toys out of common objects. He also becomes very friendly with Dr. Strong, whom he admires as a great scholar.

One day David visits Uriah Heep at his mother's for tea, not wishing to seem proud for not visiting such 'umble people. Uriah's behavior toward him is still one of obsequious deference. "There are people enough to tread upon me in my lowly state," he tells David when offered help in his law readings, "without my doing outrage to their feelings by possessing learning. Learning ain't for me. A person like myself had better not aspire."

## Comment

'Into Uriah Heep's mouth Dickens is putting the suppressed feelings of many members of the submerged lower classes of Britain, held down by social restrictions, taught to accept their humble station meekly, but seething inside with discontent and resentment. Heep does want learning (as an avenue to power), and does aspire (to Wickfield's job and daughter). His inbred hypocrisy and poisonous frustration cause near-tragedy later.

Uriah Heep's mother is a female facsimile of her son, both in appearance and behavior. She too prates constantly of humbleness and of knowing her station in life and "being thankful in it." Yet David soon becomes aware that mother and son are pumping him for every scrap of information he has about the Wickfields and their affairs. He is rescued from too many indiscreet disclosures only by the sudden appearance of his old London acquaintance, Mr. Micawber, who has seen him from the street. He meets the Heeps, addressing them with his customary grandiloquence. David goes off with Mr. Micawber to their lodgings to see Mrs. Micawber. He learns that things did not go well for them, her family having treated them coldly. They are now awaiting money from London to pay their lodging bill.

BRIGHT NOTES STUDY GUIDE

David becomes uneasy when he finds that Mr. Micawber has become friendly with the Heeps and an admirer of Uriah as a sharp young man. That night he joins the Micawbers in a convivial dinner at which Mr. Micawber is unusually jolly. He is thunderstruck when the next morning brings a note from Micawber that the debtors' prison faces him again because the expected money has not come. He is still more amazed when on going to the Micawbers' hotel he arrives just in time to see them riding off on the stagecoach, "the very picture of tranquil enjoyment ... eating walnuts out of a paper bag." A weight off his mind, David returns to school.

## CHAPTER 18: A RETROSPECT

Years have passed since the last chapter and David is now a young man of 17. He is head-boy at Dr. Strong's school, and has had a number of puppy-love affairs with girls in dancing school. He wears a gold watch, a long-tailed coat, and slicks his hair with bear's grease. Agnes Wickfield, whom he thinks of as his "sweet sister," has grown into a beautiful girl who looks just like the picture of her dead mother.

David then falls in love with Miss Larkins, a mature beauty of 30 who is much enamored of officers. He dreams of wooing and winning her despite their disparity in ages. He is lifted to the heights of romantic ecstasy when Miss Larkins after a dance gives him one of her flowers. He is in the depths of despair some time later when Miss Larkins marries a Mr. Chester, not a glamorous officer but a hop grower. These events, ruminates the adult David Copperfield, are all he remembers of his progress to the age of 17.

## Comment

With this chapter ends what many critics feel is the best part of *David Copperfield*, the account of his childhood. It is so impressive because Dickens has succeeded in evoking the world as seen through a child's eyes.

## CHAPTER 19: I LOOK ABOUT, AND MAKE A DISCOVERY

The time comes at last when David's school days are over and he must choose a profession. He has no ideas about a career, except a vague desire to lead an expedition of discovery around the world. His aunt suggests that a change of scenery and a breathing spell would do him good; he should pay an extended visit to his former haunts in London and Yarmouth. She will let him go on his own in order to let him develop his self-reliance.

Soon after, "fitted out with a handsome pursue of money, and a portmanteau," and pledging to write three times a week, David sets out on his journey. First he stops at Canterbury to say goodbye to the Wickfields. Agnes seems troubled and she confides in him that she is worried about her father. Mr. Wickfield seems haggard, has increased his port tippling, and has let it affect his business. Significantly, Uriah Heep encourages his deterioration. Stopping in at Dr. Strong's, David witnesses a discussion about a letter from Jack Maldon in India, desiring to return because of ill health. Annie's mother, "The Old Soldier," takes Jack's part and demands his return. Annie acts guilty, and David has the feeling that something is brewing of which he understands little.

## Comment

Dickens has begun to stir two sub-plots into motion. One is the domination of the Wickfields by Uriah Heep, the other the near-destruction of the Strongs' marriage by Jack Maldon (with "The Old Soldier's" connivance).

At last David is on his way to London. "The main object on my mind, I remember, ... was to appear as old as possible...." He soon realizes he is still "dreadfully young" when he is cheated out of the box seat for which he has paid on the coach. In spite of it he feels good "to be sitting up there, behind four horses: well educated, well dressed, and with plenty of money...." In London he runs into Steerforth, now an Oxford student, well dressed "with tasteful easy negligence" and as handsome as ever. Steerforth, calling David "Daisy" for his innocent naivete, promises to take him under his wing and make him more sophisticated.

## CHAPTER 20: STEERFORTH'S HOME

David and Steerforth breakfast together the next morning. David is dazzled by Steerforth's suave, worldly manner, but surprised that he does not intend to get a degree at the university. "Why should I trouble myself, that a parcel of heavy-headed fellows may gape ...?" he asks. Steerforth takes David with him to visit his mother at Highgate, just outside London. She lives in an old-fashioned brick house with another lady, her companion, a Miss Rosa Dartle. David is intrigued by Miss Dartle, a thin woman with black hair, gaunt black eyes, and a scar upon her lip. She seems consumed by "the effect of some wasting fire within her," and she takes pleasure in indirectly contradicting people. Steerforth tells David that it was he who had inflicted the scar when as a boy he had thrown a hammer at her in a temper tantrum.

David asks Steerforth to join him on his coming visit to the Peggottys in Yarmouth. Steerforth assents, saying it would be amusing "to see that sort of people together." David is bewildered by the attitude toward his old friends displayed in the conversation of these upper-class people. Are the Peggottys "really animals and clods, and beings of a lower order," who "under their coarse rough skins ... are not easily wounded"?

## Comment

In displaying the heartless class snobbery of Steerforth and Rosa Dartle toward the Peggottys, Dickens is laying a finger on one of the festering sores of his society. He himself as the son of so-called "lower-class" parents had doubtlessly felt this snobbery turned on him more than once. Yet, strangely, Dickens (as David Copperfield) is a snob in turn when later he calls the charity-school-bred Uriah "a red-haired animal." Remember also David's shame at being forced to work in the warehouse with "that sort of company."

David spends a few days in this strange household, and is made very welcome by Mrs. Steerforth because he is such an admirer of her son. She is devoted to Steerforth, treasuring locks of his hair and every letter he ever wrote to her. Her possessive love can allow her to see no mark of imperfection in him. Her idolatry and indulgence have made him the flawed character he is. Rosa Dartle, too, loves Steerforth, but secretly, and her smoldering passion has a sick quality to it. David senses this queer emotional turbulence as he spends the first night under their roof.

## Comment

Dickens again shows himself a master of psychological insights. The love of Mrs. Steerforth for her son (a substitute for her dead husband) is almost incestuous in its intensity. Rosa Dartle's love also has a psychotic quality to it, for she is much older than Steerforth and she regards his mother as a rival for his love.

## CHAPTER 21: LITTLE EM'LY

David's visit with the Steerforths lingers on into a week. He is ministered to by Steerforth's man-servant Littimer, who awes David with his imperturbable air of respectability. Under his friend's tutelage, David has lessons in horsemanship, fencing, and boxing. His admiration of the lordly Steerforth grows and he even finds agreeable "his dashing way ... of treating me like a plaything."

At last they go down together to Yarmouth, where David is to renew old memories. Everything looks smaller, but then David reflects, things "that we have only seen as children always do...." Omer's shop, where he had once been measured for a suit of mourning, was now "Omer and Joram." Mr. Omer tells David that Little Em'ly works for him as a dressmaker. Em'ly does not mix much with the other girls, and still talks of someday being a lady. David sees that she is beautiful, with "the old capricious coyness" still in her face.

Next he stops in at the Barkis house, but Peggotty, whom he has not seen for ten years, does not recognize him at first. They have a heartfelt reunion, laughter mingling with tears. She takes him upstairs to see Barkis, who is now a rheumatic invalid but who gives him an enthusiastic welcome. Steerforth, too, when he arrives is made welcome and endears himself to the couple. The two young men continue on to the Peggotty houseboat that evening. Crossing the flats on the way, Steerforth remarks that "the sea roars as if it were hungry for us."

## Comment

Dickens again foreshadows coming events. He telegraphs his literary punches, as it were, too often for modern tastes, but it was necessary for the manner of novel he wrote. Little Em'ly's often-repeated wish to be a lady (to rise above her station) is what leads her to seduction by Steerforth. And Steerforth, talking about the roar of the hungry sea, is prophesying his own death off this very shore.

They arrive at the Peggotty home just in time to hear of the engagement of Little Em'ly to Ham. The scene is joyous, with even old Mrs. Gummidge jolted out of her usual despondency. Mr. Peggotty states that he can now die easy, knowing that Ham will always be there to look after Em'ly. Steerforth makes a complimentary speech, but privately tells the shocked David that he considers Ham "too chuckleheaded" for her. The naive David does not yet see that Steerforth really despises these people and is only playing a game with them.

## Comment

Because of Steerforth, who meets Em'ly at the moment of her engagement to Ham, the marriage never takes place.

# DAVID COPPERFIELD

. . . . . . . . . . . . . . . . . . . . . . . . . . . . . . . . . . . . . . . . . . . . . . . . . . . . . . . . . .

## CHAPTER 22: SOME OLD SCENES, AND SOME NEW PEOPLE

David and Steerforth spend two weeks in Yarmouth. Steerforth often goes boating with Mr. Peggotty, for "his restless nature and bold spirits delighted to find a vent in rough toil and hard weather," and he often stands treat to the sailors in the local tavern. David visits his old home, Blunderstone, now dilapidated and occupied "only by a poor lunatic gentleman." Doctor Chillip he finds remarried to "a tall, raw-boned highnosed wife." He is saddened by all the decay and change in the old neighborhood.

When he meets Steerforth that night, he finds him sitting lost in meditation before fire at the Peggotty house, alone. Steerforth seems melancholy and disturbed about something. "I wish to God I had had a judicious father these last twenty years," he tells David. "I wish with all my soul I could guide myself better!" But he won't tell David what troubles him. Instead he announces that he has bought a boat, a clipper which will be renamed "Little Em'ly" and which Mr. Peggotty will skipper when Steerforth is away. Littimer, the "respectable" servant, is coming down to see to the boat's outfitting.

## Comment

Even the villain-to-be, Steerforth, is permitted by Dickens to have his periods of remorse and self-realization. In this **episode** Steerforth blames his weakness, his lack of moral self-control on not having had a father. It is strange that the novel's other villain, Uriah Heep, likewise lacks a father.

One day David and Steerforth are visited by Miss Mowcher, a misshapen dwarf-woman who was well-known in fashionable circles as a hairdresser and accomplice in intrigues. David is impressed by her name-dropping of Princes and Dukes while she works on Steerforth's hair. She seems rather interested in their descriptions of the beautiful Em'ly. Again Steerforth says that Em'ly is "throwing herself away ... I swear she was born to be a lady."

## Comment

Miss Mowcher, the dwarf hairdresser, was based on an actual woman Dickens knew. He meant to make her one of the evil helpers of Steerforth, a procuress who arranges his sexual escapades perhaps. But the real-life Miss Mowcher protested, and Dickens turned her into a heroine later on.

Another odd confrontation occurs when David at the Barkis house meets Martha Endell, a girl who once worked with Em'ly at Omer's but who has become a "fallen woman." She wants to go to London and start life over where no one knows her. Em'ly and Ham help her with money. When she is gone, Em'ly cries out to Ham, "I am not as good a girl as I ought to be ... it might have been a better fortune for you, if you had been fond of someone else...." But Ham takes her in his arms and comforts her.

## Comment

Like Steerforth, Em'ly, who has begun a secret affair with him, (we must guess between the lines) is stricken with guilt and remorse. Martha is the living warning of what she will be if she succumbs. Dickens has set all the machinery of impending tragedy in motion.

## CHAPTER 23: I CORROBORATE MR. DICK, AND CHOOSE A PROFESSION

David receives a letter from his aunt reminding him that he is to choose a profession when he has vacationed enough. She suggests that he become a proctor, but David has to ask Steerforth what a proctor is. He is told that it is a sort of lawyer, one who specializes in wills, marriages, and nautical disputes, a lucrative if somewhat dull profession. They ride into London, where David is to meet his aunt.

David meets Aunt Betsey at her lodgings and expresses his delight at her suggestion of a profession. He worries that it will be too expensive for her; a thousand pounds is the fee to be articled in a law firm. She reassures him that as his guardian she will gladly pay the sum, for he has ever been a credit to her. "Only be a loving child to me in my age, and bear with my whims and fancies," she pleads.

They are on the way to the law firm where David is to be articled, when his aunt is accosted by "a lowering ill-dressed man," a beggar David thinks, but his aunt is strangely disturbed. As she drives off with the man, David remembers Mr. Dick's story of the mysterious stranger, which he had thought a hallucination. When his aunt returns a little later, she begs him not to discuss the matter, and he finds that she has been relieved of considerable money.

## Comment

By now every reader should have guessed that the stranger is Aunt Betsey's long-lost husband, come back to blackmail her.

At Spenlow and Jorkins, the law-firm, David meets Mr. Spenlow, one of the partners, "a little light-haired gentleman" who "must have taken a great deal of pains with his whiskers," dressed stiffly and wearing a massive gold watch chain. They encounter difficulties in making the arrangements for David, for Mr. Jorkins, the absent partner, is supposed to be "the most obdurate and ruthless of men" who wouldn't hear of terms less than a month's probation without salary. David later finds that the real Jorkins, a mild-mannered man, is used as a terrifying figurehead to cow people with.

One more arrangement needs to be made. Lodgings for David are found at the house of Mrs. Crupp, "a stout lady with a flounce of flannel petticoat below a nankeen gown." The "chambers," consisting of a pantry, a sitting-room, and a bedroom, all with rather faded furniture, but with a view of the river, impress David as cozy, if not sumptuous. He feels dignified to have "chambers" of his own.

## CHAPTER 24: MY FIRST DISSIPATION

Soon the joy of having a place of his own palls on David, and it becomes rather dreary, especially as he hasn't seen Steerforth since he has come to London. He is therefore happy when Steerforth suddenly appears one day, and to celebrate, David arranges for a house-warming dinner party that night. Mrs. Crupp, he finds, cannot cook or serve the dinner, so it must be ordered from a pastry cook's restaurant. Besides, she will need two helpers to do it in style. David assents to all her demands, and goes out to order wine.

That night, Steerforth, who brings two friends, takes the head of the table and presides over the festivities. Innumerable toasts are drunk, there is much smoking, and David, unused to either, soon finds himself feeling queer. The party breaks up when someone suggests they go to the theater. On the way out David is surprised to find that it was he who fell down the stairs. At the theater, which is hot and stuffy, he is unable to understand what is going on upon the stage, for the whole place seems to be swimming Downstairs in one of the boxes, he meets Agnes Wickfield, who looks at him with hurt amazement. She tells him to have his friends take him home.

The next morning he awakes with a terrible hangover, tortured by remorse and shame for his first dissipation.

## CHAPTER 25: GOOD AND BAD ANGELS

A few days after his first (and last) dissipation, David receives a note, brought by a porter, from Agnes Wickfield. She is staying at the house of her father's London agent, a Mr. Waterbrook, and wants to see him. In his reply he first wants to apologize for his disreputable conduct at the theater, but he changes his mind. When a little later he sees her in person, he breaks down in tears of self-reproach. "If it had been any one but you ... who saw me," he cries. "You are my good angel." Agnes replies that she wishes to warn him against his bad angel, Steerforth. David denies that Steerforth's influence is bad for him, but Agnes fears that he is a dangerous friend.

## Comment

Dickens from the first portrays Agnes as a superior creature. In the beginning she is the efficient "little housekeeper," now she is a wise young woman who has penetrated Steerforth's disguised character. In fact she seems to be the only one not taken in by his ingratiating glamor.

Agnes tells David that Uriah Heep is often in London on business and that he is about to become her father's law-partner. "What," cries David indignantly, "That mean, fawning fellow, worm himself into such promotion!" Uriah, she tells him, has made himself indispensable to Mr. Wickfield, preying on his weakness, until now he has power over him. Agnes begs David to be friendly to Uriah, not to resent or repel him, because the antagonism might hurt her or her father.

At a dinner party with the Waterbrooks the next day, David comes face to face with Uriah Heep dressed "in a suit of black and in deep humility." He notices the "shadowless eyes and cadaverous face" of Uriah watching him all evening, especially when he is with Agnes.

A happier reunion is that with Tommy Traddles, his chubby one-time schoolmate at Salem House, Creakle's favorite whipping-boy. It turns out that Mr. Waterbrook, for whom Traddles works, has only invited him because another guest couldn't come. The dinner party itself is a dull affair with the stuffed-shirt guests vying to out-brag each other about their social connections, professional importance, and reverence for "the Blood."

On the way home David finds Uriah behind him, and for Agnes's sake he invites him up to his chambers for tea. Uriah professes to be greatly honored and is profusely grateful for the invitation. But as they sit over their cups, Uriah reveals his growing sense of power. Mr. Wickfield has been imprudent, and he, Uriah, has saved him from ruin, he hints. "I have risen from my umble station ... but I am umble still," he assures David. It is hard for David to hold himself in check when Uriah confides that he worships Agnes. "She is much attached to her father ... that I think she may come, on his account, to be kind to me." Uriah begs David to keep it a secret that he expects to marry Agnes someday. The vision of the slimy Uriah married to Agnes is too repulsive to contemplate. But worse is in store, for Uriah insists on staying the night in David's quarters, sleeping on the sofa. In the morning David requests Mrs. Crupp to make sure his rooms are well aired to be "purged of Uriah's presence."

## Comment

The sweet young girl threatened by a scheming villain has always been the stock-in-trade of melodrama. The subplot of the machinations of Heep, involving the Wickfields, Micawbers (and Betsey Trotwood as well) is coming rapidly to a boil.

## CHAPTER 26: I FALL INTO CAPTIVITY

David sees Agnes and the detestable Uriah off on the stage back to Canterbury. He realizes that Agnes has accepted Uriah's usurpation because she loves her father and thinks she is the cause of his weakness. David worries about her future: "Hardly a night passed without my dreaming of it," he writes.

The weeks slip by and David is finally articled to Spenlow and Jorkins. The evenings are dreary. Mrs. Crupp, his landlady, suffers from "the spazzums." David drinks coffee by the gallon and writes poetry bemoaning his solitude. At last there is a break in the monotony of his life when Mr. Spenlow asks him to spend a weekend at his house in the country. He is a widower and his daughter has just returned from finishing school in Paris. David is the envy of the other clerks for this invitation, as the Spenlow mansion to them is a place of grandeur and mystery.

## Comment

Note that Dora Spenlow, like Agnes and Little Em'ly, the other heroines in the novel, has no mother. The villains, Steerforth and Heep, have no fathers. This is more than a coincidence, but the psychological implications are obscure.

On the trip down, in a very handsome carriage (a status symbol among lawyers, David guesses), Mr. Spenlow discusses with David his future profession. When they arrive, David is enchanted with the house, the gardens, and most of all, with the curly-haired beauty, Miss Dora Spenlow. "I was swallowed up in an abyss of love in an instant," he recalls. He is brought back to earth out of the clouds of instant love by hearing a familiar, if odious, voice. It is that of Miss Murdstone, his ancient adversary of Blunderstone days. She is now the "confidential friend" of Dora, really her paid companion or chaperone. Privately, he and Miss Murdstone agree to an armistice and not to reveal their past relationship to others. But before they agree, David has the satisfaction of telling her what he thinks of her for the past.

## Comment

The reappearance of Miss Murdstone is typical of the too-well-knit plots of Victorian novels. There are just too many coincidences of this type to suit the more realistic-minded reader of today. Real life is never this neat.

David is delirious in his infatuation, extending his affection even to Dora's little black dog Jip. He spends a wonderful weekend, even enjoying the Sunday church service although Miss Murdstone sits between Dora and him. Even when he returns to the everyday world of law courts and dreary admiralty cases, he is still in a daze. He takes to wearing straw-colored gloves and shoes that are much too tight, and becomes extravagant, buying sumptuous waistcoats. He rarely gets a glimpse of Dora and is disappointed in not being invited to Spenlow's again.

Mrs. Crupp, his landlady, is sympathetic to his romantic woes. She advises him to "cheer up, sir, to keep a good heart … and to take up skittles" ( a form of bowling).

## Comment

The account of David's first real love affair, which begins in this chapter, is one of heart-warming tenderness. Dickens is really reliving his own youthful love affair with Maria Beadnell, but Maria was capricious, her father unrelenting, and they never married. Now he triumphs in the person of David.

## CHAPTER 27: TOMMY TRADDLES

One day David looks up his old Salem School friend, Tommy Traddles. Searching for the house, he wanders through a run-down section of the city with garbage in the streets. It all somehow recalls his own days with the Micawbers, even to the milkman loudly demanding payment at the door of the Tradle'es place. He finds Traddles at home in his little room, surrounded by a few poor belongings, reading law. "I ... am fighting my way on in the world against difficulties, and it would be ridiculous if I made a pretense of doing anything else," he tells David.

They reminisce about old schooldays under the cruel Creakle, and Traddles tells David how after the death of the uncle whose heir he thought he was, he found himself cut off in the will. Since then he has made his own way, copying out wills and such for Mr. Waterbrook, and studying for the bar exam. He faces the world cheerfully and has even become engaged to the daughter of a curate. She is one of ten daughters, older than he, and is patiently willing to wait "till she was sixty" for him. With pride Traddles shows David the things they have already collected for their future home, a flower stand and a little table.

David is surprised to see that Traddles' landlord is Mr. Micawber, optimistic and grandiloquent as ever. His wife is, as usual, expecting, and he is in his customary financial difficulties, but is hoping for "something to turn up." David refuses an invitation to dine with the Micawbers (to Mrs.

Micawber's visible relief) and invites them to dine with him in a few days. Then he takes his leave.

## Comment

In the portraits of Traddleses and the Micawbers, Dickens is picturing people close to his heart - the poor, cheerfully struggling on the fringes of society. These types are always drawn with sympathy, while upper-class characters are often the butt of **satire** (as at the Waterbrooks' dinner). In bringing together Traddles and Micawber, he is putting in place a link in the Heep-Wickfield subplot. It is this team, the ingenuous Traddles and the improvident Micawber, which will thwart the schemes of the evil Uriah Heep.

## CHAPTER 28: MR. MICAWBER'S GAUNTLET

When the day comes in which David is to give the dinner party for his "newly-found old friends," Mrs. Crupp balks at preparing even the simple meal has planned. She agrees to cook the fish and small leg of mutton only if he will eat out for the two weeks following. David, ever tyrannized by Mrs. Crupp, consents to her terms.

The Micawbers and Traddleses come, and are delighted with his chambers. Mr. Micawber is soon at work preparing a bowl of rum punch. "I never saw a man so thoroughly enjoy himself amid the fragrance of lemon-peel and sugar, the odour of burning rum, and the steam of boiling water ...," writes David. Yet Micawber has just had his water turned off for non-payment. When the dinner is served it turns out to be a disappointment. The leg mutton is half raw because Mrs. Crupp had been taken by "the spazzums" before it was done. The pigeon pie is "full of lumps and bumps, with nothing particular underneath." Mr. Micawber turns tragedy into triumph by having the mutton sliced, grilled, and served with mushroom ketchup of his wife's invention. In the enjoyment of this improvised meal, David even "forgot Dora for a little while."

## Comment

In each of Dickens' novels there are a number of scenes like this. He delighted to show a convivial group eating and drinking together. Again he is making up for what he did not have in his own life.

Littimer, Steerworth's man servant, suddenly appears, looking for his master. Utterly "respectable," he takes over the serving of the grilled lamb, discomposing the party by his expertness. David feels ill at ease, and he has a vague suspicion about Steerforth's whereabouts.

After Littimer leaves, the party resumes its former jolliness. Mr. Micawber tells David of his plans for the future, he not having met success as either a coal or corn salesman. Mrs. Micawber, in a long, passionate speech, declares that Mr. Micawber, a man of great talents, has just not been discovered by those who could use him. He should therefore "throw the gauntlet" to society by advertising himself in the newspaper. The considerable expense of this venture could be met by a promissory note.

## Comment

Although the devotion of Mrs. Micawber for her improvident husband is treated with comic touches, Dickens obviously wants to us to admire her. "I will never desert Mr. Micawber," is her battle cry. Dickens, whose own domestic life was unsatisfactory, envies the Micawbers for their loyalty and devotion to each other in spite of adversity.

On the way out, David quietly warns Traddles not to get into Micawber's difficulties by signing any bills for him, but it is too late. Traddles has already signed.

The party of guests is hardly out the door when Steerforth appears, bearing a letter from Peggotty. He has been at Yarmouth doing some sailing and having "an escapade of a week or two." The letter from Peggotty bears bad news; Barkis is dying. David feels he should go down to offer his help and solace, but he is first asked by Steerforth to spend a day with him and his mother at Highgate. Before retiring for the night after this busy day, David reads a note left him by Micawber. That gentleman's goods have been seized for non-payment of rent, and those of the unfortunate Traddles, his boarder, as well. That Mr. Micawber would recover from this financial blow, David knew, but what about poor Traddles and his long-waiting vicar's daughter, one of ten?

## CHAPTER 29: I VISIT STEERFORTH AT HIS HOME, AGAIN

David is given permission by Mr. Spenlow to take time off from his not-yet arduous (or paid) duties. He rides out to Highgate, where both Mrs. Steerforth and Rosa Dartle seem glad to see him again. But he notices that Rosa searches him out with "the lynx-like scrutiny" of her "gaunt black eyes." She tries to pry out of him information (which he does not have) about the goings and comings of Steerforth. "What is he doing?" she asks him. "In what manner is that man assisting him ...?"

## Comment

Rosa Dartle (like the reader by now) suspects that Steerforth is up to something, involved in some sinister escapade, helped by Littimer, his servant. She thinks that David, as his friend, knows about it.

Steerforth turns his charm upon Rosa Dartle with full force and manages to get her to play the harp and sing for them. David is enthralled by the music, but finds the song "most unearthly ... sprung out of the passion within her...." Steerforth puts his arm around her and tells her, "Come, Rosa, for the future we will love each other very much!" She strikes him and stalks out of the room furiously. The puzzled David later asks Steerforth about her behavior and is told, "She is an edge-tool, and requires great care in dealing with. She is always dangerous."

## Comment

The strange behavior of Rosa Dartle is caused by her insanely jealous love for Steerforth. He senses it and callously plays with it, provoking the outburst.

As David expects to leave for Yarmouth before Steerforth gets up the next morning, he says goodbye before going to bed. Steerforth puts his hands on David's shoulders affectionately and says, "Think of me at my best, if circumstances should ever part us." In the morning he peeks into Steerforth's room and sees him asleep, resting his head on his arm just as he used to do at school. David is never to see him again.

## CHAPTER 30: A LOSS

Arriving at Yarmouth, David stops off at Omer and Joram's (the undertaker, draper, tailor, etc.) to get some news. Mr. Omer tells him that Barkis is close to death. David asks about Little Em'ly and is told that she seems "unsettled" lately about something. Mr. Omer adds, "I shall be glad when her marriage has taken place."

When David gets to the Barkis house he finds Peggotty and her family all gathered there. Little Em'ly is clinging to her uncle and David notices that her hand is cold and trembling when he takes it. Mr. Peggotty excuses her, saying that it is only natural for one like Em'ly to be affected by the nearness of death. Upstairs Peggotty shows David to Barkis, who is lying on his bed, protectively hovering over his mysterious box. "He's a going out with the tide," says Mr. Peggotty. "People can't die along the coast except when the tide's pretty nigh out." Barkis regains consciousness a minute, long enough to recognize David and murmur, "Barkis is willin'!" Then he goes out with the tide.

## Comment

In this short chapter (originally written as part of the next chapter) Dickens is concluding one of the minor subplots - the Peggotty-Barkis romance - and setting up the **climax** of the Steerforth-Little Em'ly plot. The death of Barkis is done in a subdued tone rather than in the usual exaggerated fashion. But then Barkis was a subdued, rather taciturn man.

## CHAPTER 31: A GREATER LOSS

After David has seen the remains of Barkis laid to rest in Blunderstone churchyard (where his own parents were buried), he takes a professional interest in settling Peggotty's affairs. The mysterious box which Barkis had never let out of his sight all these years is opened. It contains not only a will but an odd assortment of things: a silver tobacco stopper, an imitation lemon, a piece of camphor, and some money. Barkis, always thrifty, has left almost three thousand pounds. Peggotty is the biggest beneficiary, of course, but Mr. Peggotty, Little Em'ly, and even David, are also marked for bequests.

## Comment

The money which the unsuspecting Peggotty inherits from Barkis will later help Betsey Trotwood when she has lost her fortune. The women, both in a sense David's substitute mothers, are thus united.

The evening after the funeral, David goes to the Peggotty house. He finds the family gathered there waiting for Em'ly to come home. After a few words about Barkis and Peggotty, "She done her dooty by the departed; and the departed know'd it," the conversation turns to Em'ly. Mr. Peggotty already mourns the time after her marriage when he will wait for her in vain to come home. She is more than a daughter to him.

The door opens, but it is Ham who enters, not Em'ly. He asks David to step outside a moment. There he tells him, "Em'ly's run away!" He doesn't know how to break the news to the others. David reads a note Em'ly has left to the assembled family. "When I leave my dear home in the morning," she wrote, "... it will be never to come back, unless he brings me back a lady." She admits her wrongdoing and is sorry to hurt those she loves and who love her, especially Mr. Peggotty and Ham. "... Try to think as if I had died when I was little and was buried somewhere," she concludes. Mr. Peggotty with torn vest and blood trickling from his mouth is almost beside himself with grief and shock. "Who's the man? I want to know his name," he demands wildly. Bit by bit the story comes out that a servant has been seen lurking about, a strange horse and carriage seen driving down the road shortly after daybreak. The man is Steerforth.

Mr. Peggotty wants to run out immediately in pursuit. "I'm going to seek my niece through the wureld. I'm a going to find my poor niece in her shame, and bring her back. No one stop me!" he cries. Mrs. Gummidge, always the querulous old whiner, now reveals a calm and fortitude which soothe Mr. Peggotty. David is deeply affected by this terrible turn of events. "My overcharged heart found ... relief, and I cried too," he writes.

## Comment

This is the **climax** of the Steerforth-Little Em'ly plot, a scene described with unrestrained emotion. All is very carefully calculated by the author to call forth manifold emotional reactions on the parts of various classes of readers. A "poor but honest" girl has been seduced by a "rich but rotten" young man. A trusting bridegroom has been deceived and jilted. A closely-knit family has been cruelly shattered. A friend has been used and betrayed. Almost every reader can put himself into at least one of these categories. This close identification helps explain the immense popularity of Dickens.

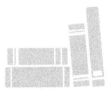

# DAVID COPPERFIELD

....................................................................

### CHAPTER 32: THE BEGINNING OF A LONG JOURNEY

David reproaches himself that he is responsible for the family's sorrow, for he had introduced Steerforth to Em'ly. He resolves to think of Steerforth as "a cherished friend, who was dead." Mr. Peggotty has calmed down and decided to search the world for Em'ly and bring her back, Mrs. Gummidge is to remain behind in the familiar houseboat to keep things ready for Em'ly's return. In Ham's face David notes "an expression of stern determination ... that if he ever encountered Steerforth, he would kill him."

### Comment

Rather than kill Steerforth, Ham ironically dies trying to save him (but not knowing who it is). In this section Ham is also allowed a premonition of his death. Steerforth has had his premonition earlier, you remember.

The reaction of the people in the neighborhood is mixed. "Many were hard on her, some few were hard upon him," David notes, but all felt sorrow for Ham and Mr. Peggotty. Mr. Joram calls Em'ly "a deceitful, bad-hearted girl," but he doesn't mean it.

David is sitting up late one night at Peggotty's when he hears a knock on the door. It is a huge umbrella with Miss Mowcher, the dwarf hairdresser, under it. She has hurried down to Yarmouth to warn of the elopement. She had known of the intrigue for some time, but had been deceived into thinking that it was David, not Steerforth who was after the girl. She admits that she had acted as go-between, passing on a letter to Em'ly. "I have some reason to suspect," she tells David, "that they are gone abroad." She will find out what she can about them through her many connections. For Littimer, Steerforth's sly but "respectable" servant who has screened his master's intentions from her, she reserves a special hatred. "And Littimer had better have a bloodhound at his back, than little Mowcher!" she vows.

## Comment

Miss Mowcher, in this her second appearance, has been made over into one of the "good" characters. We can admire Dickens' art in this **episode**, in explaining away her previous behavior. It is a foregone conclusion that Miss Mowcher will track down Littimer. Poetic justice (and the long arm of coincidence) must be served.

The next morning David and Mr. Peggotty ride off to London to see Steerforth's mother. She knows what has happened and sits in her chair pale and "with a stately, immovable, passionless air." Mr. Peggotty asks her if Steerforth will keep his word to bring Em'ly back a lady, that is, to marry her. Mrs. Steerforth replies that it is impossible. "You cannot fail to know that she is far below him," she says frigidly. "Such a marriage would irretrievably blight my son's career, and ruin his prospects." She grows angry at the thought of the injury done to her by her son. She had done everything for him, and he has "set this wretched fancy" above her. Rosa Dartle, who catches them on their way out, is even more vehement in her emotional outbursts. Although she admits that Steerforth "has a false, corrupt heart," she feels no pity for Em'ly or Mr. Peggotty. "They are a depraved, worthless set. I would have her whipped," she hisses to David. "I would have her branded on the face, drest in rags, and cast out in the streets to starve."

## Comment

In picturing the various reactions to the elopement, Dickens again displays keen psychological insights. The Peggottys pity her for the disgrace she has brought on herself, not on them. Their feelings are thus basically unselfish (even those of Ham, the left-in-the-lurch bridegroom). In contrast, Mrs. Steerforth is aghast at the injury done to herself, that her much-indulged son should have taken up with a common girl. Rosa Dartle's reaction is also in tune with her hate-love relationship to Steerforth. She knows he is corrupt, but she can't stand to see another woman have him.

## CHAPTER 33: BLISSFUL

"All this time, I had gone on loving Dora, harder than ever," David writes. "The greater the accumulation of deceit and trouble in the world, the brighter and purer shone the star of Dora high above the world." He sneaks about her house at night, "blowing kisses at the lights in the window," and generally behaving as silly as young men in love usually do.

In the meantime David has arranged for the settlement of Peggotty's legal affairs with the Legacy Office. While waiting to pay the fee for these services, Peggotty and David are surprised to see Mr. Murdstone, the terror of David's youth, come in with Mr. Spenlow. Their meeting is chilly; old animosities and accusations are exchanged. Later from Mr. Spenlow David hears that Murdstone has just taken out a license to marry again; "a rather good marriage ... I understand there's money. Beauty too," he says. The girl, an heiress, has just turned 21 and Murdstone has been waiting for her to come of age.

## Comment

The novel now turns again to the affairs of the central character. The reappearance of Murdstone is another one of those improbable coincidences so loved by the Victorian audience. Of course they anticipate that Murdstone will treat his new wife as cruelly as he had David's mother.

David by now has accustomed himself to the routine of affairs in legal Commons, and Mr. Spenlow is beginning to treat him as a colleague. Mr. Spenlow in his conversations is revealed as a conservative old gentleman to whom any change or reform in the institution of laws would signal the fall of the nation itself. "He considered it the principle of a gentleman to take things as he found them," David writes.

## Comment

One strain of **satire** in this novel is leveled at the law and lawyers. The law, according to Dickens, does not administer justice or regulate human affairs, but lives only to perpetuate itself as an institution and provide good livings for those who work in it. In a later novel, *Bleak House*, Dickens was to turn his full fury on the institution of laws, courts, and lawyers.

Mr. Spenlow invites the overjoyed David to a picnic to celebrate David's birthday. Equipped with new (and very tight boots, a loud cravat, a bouquet, and on a gallant horse, David rides to the Spenlow house in Norwood. He finds Dora in the garden with the dog Jip, and a friend, Miss Julia Mills. At the picnic, to his chagrin, Dora is taken in tow by an obnoxious rival with red whiskers. David, pained with jealousy, flirts with a girl in pink. Miss Mills, who at 20 is an experienced hand in love affairs (having recently gone through one), arranges a quick reconciliation. Better yet, she invites David to come to her house when Dora will be staying with her.

Before he makes his visit, David determines that the time has come to tell Dora of his love and to get her answer. Miss Mills soon leaves the lovers alone and David, after some hesitation, proposes to Dora. At last he has declared his passion. "It was off my mind. I was in a state of perfect rapture," he writes. Dora tells him that she will never marry him without her father's consent, but they decide to keep their intentions a secret for awhile. Thinking back on his early love, David writes, "What an unsubstantial, happy, foolish time! Of all the times of mine that Time has in his grip, there is none that in one retrospect I can smile at half so much, and think of half so tenderly."

## Comment

In this idyllic picture of young love with its tenderness and silliness mingled, Dickens is reliving his own love affair with Maria Beadnell, probably as a reaction to his growing estrangement with his wife, Kate.

## CHAPTER 34: MY AUNT ASTONISHES ME

As soon as Dora and David are engaged, he announces the news in a letter to Agnes. He assures her that this is a deep, abiding passion, not a boyish fancy, and he visualizes her reading this with her clear eyes in the so-gentle face.

Meanwhile David is caught up in the growing feud between Peggotty and Mrs. Crupp, his landlady, who resents the presence of "intruders and informers, especially in widders' weeds." The stairways are lined with pitchers as pitfalls to induce Peggotty to break her legs, but David is too afraid of Mrs. Crupp to remonstrate.

When Traddles comes to call, David tells him of his engagement. Poor Traddles envies David because Dora is so close by and his Sophy, one of ten daughters of a vicar in Devonshire, is so far away. Traddles also tells David that he no longer lives with the Micawbers. That gentleman, in financial difficulties again, has changed his name to Mortimer, donned glasses as a disguise and goes out only after dark. Although the trousseau flower-pot and little table are in the hands of a pawnbroker from the last time, Traddles has again foolishly co-signed a note for Mr. Micawber. After warning Traddles strongly to lend Micawber neither money nor his name in the future, David arranges to redeem the flower pot and table. Peggotty and David return to his chambers. On the way upstairs they notice that the pitcher-pitfalls have been removed and that his door stands open. Great is their amazement to see inside his aunt, Betsey Trotwood, sitting on a pile of luggage, with Mr. Dick leaning nearby on a huge kite. Before Aunt Betsey has offered a single word of explanation, in her usual commanding way she has renamed Peggotty (that South Sea island name) to Barkis, and has quelled the officious Mrs. Crupp. Then she tells her story. "Trot, have you got to be firm and self-reliant?" she asks. "I am ruined, my dear Trot ... We must meet reverses boldly, and not suffer them to frighten us my dear."

## Comment

This chapter marks a turn in events. The money which supported him after his first reversal of fortune (his mother's death and his flight from the London warehouse) is now gone. He must stand upon his own two feet, relying entirely upon himself, with no one to turn to for help this time.

## CHAPTER 35: DEPRESSION

As soon as David recovers his presence of mind he makes housing arrangements for Mr. Dick. His aunt is to occupy his bed and he is to sleep in the sitting room. Aunt Betsey takes a liking for Peggotty, "Barkis" now, and she in turn has offered her money to Aunt Betsey. Aunt Betsey has heard all about Dora too. "So you fancy yourself in love! Do you?" she asks. "And so you think you were formed for one another, and are to go through a party-supper-table kind of life, like two pretty pieces of confectionery, do you, Trot?" What he needs, she adds, is someone to sustain him and improve him. He is blind to think otherwise. David feels vaguely depressed by this.

## Comment

This is the first hint that Dora is not the wife for David. We shall see later that she is indeed "lightheaded" and does not have the qualities to "sustain and improve him." But he has to find this out for himself.

David worries what his financial reverses will do to his romance as well as his career. He has fitful dreams of abject poverty that night. In the morning he goes in to Mr. Spenlow to tell him his troubles and to get back at least a part of the thousand-pound fee paid for his law-apprenticeship. Mr. Spenlow responds with sympathy but refers him to that mythical tyrant, his partner Mr. Jorkins. That gentleman, a mild little man in reality, refers him back to Spenlow. The upshot is that no money will be returned, and David, sunk in gloom, leaves the office. On the street he is overtaken by a coach and he sees "the face ... never seen without a feeling of serenity and happiness.... " It is Agnes Wickfield. She has come to London with her father and Uriah Heep, now his full partner. She tells David that the Heeps have moved into the Wickfield house, in fact Uriah sleeps in David's old room. The Heeps manage to keep her apart from her father most of the time, but she hopes that she will be able to help him resist Uriah.

When Agnes and David join Aunt Betsey in his lodgings, they talk about how they are to manage financially. The Spenlow position pays no salary as yet and they must have money to live. Agnes mentions that Dr. Strong, now retired, is looking for a part-time secretary. David promptly arranges for an interview with his old Canterbury master.

## Comment

David is about to begin a new career. The career of David from now on rather closely resembles the real-life career of Charles Dickens.

## CHAPTER 36: ENTHUSIASM

David has come to terms with the changed circumstances of his life and is no longer dispirited. He wants to show his aunt that her past support of him "had not been thrown away on an insensible, ungrateful object" and that he is able "to work with a resolute and steady heart." His goal is not only to help his aunt but to win Dora in spite of his reverses of fortune.

He goes to see Dr. Strong, who now lives in an old but substantial cottage in Highgate. The good Doctor is glad to see him, now that he is grown to manhood. He tells David that his wife, Annie, is well and that her mother, Mrs. Markleham, has had Jack Maldon brought back from India and had him set up in a little patent office of his own. When David asks him for the part-time secretary job, the Doctor is first hesitant because the pay, seventy-pounds per year, is so low. But David tells him of his needs and the Doctor accepts him. The work, a few hours in the morning and evening, is not onerous, but consists of helping the doctor with his dictionary project of so many years' standing.

## Comment

In bringing David together again with Dr. Strong, Dickens enables us to watch the development of another subplot, that involving Dr. Strong, Annie Strong and Jack Maldon.

David goes to visit Traddles, taking Mr. Dick with him. He wants to find some employment for that amiable dim-wit, and Traddles puts Mr. Dick to work copying out legal documents. David also wants information on the possibilities of entering the newspaper world as a parliamentary reporter, a profession that had attracted him lately. Traddles tells him that this career is especially difficult because it takes many years to learn shorthand. David is not discouraged, but determines that this is the profession for him.

A note comes from Mr. Micawber, stating that at last "something had turned up," and that he is soon to leave London. David visits the Micawbers to say farewell, finds them packed and ready to leave for Canterbury, their new field of endeavor. The gauntlet which he had so nobly flung down to society in an advertisement, has been taken up, states Micawber. David is surprised to hear that the new employer is none other than Uriah Heep, for whom Micawber is to function as confidential clerk. The Micawbers are in their usual state of enthusiastic optimism, already seeing Mr. Micawber culminating a great law career as a magistrate. After all, hasn't Mr. Micawber had vast experience with the law? (As defendant, of course!) David wishes the Micawbers well in their new life, but is privately rather disturbed by the Heep-Micawber connection.

## Comment

Dickens is stirring another sub-plot, the affairs of the Heeps and the Wickfields, into renewed activity. Micawber as Heep's confidential clerk gets to know his affairs and eventually is instrumental in unmasking the villain. Dickens, in a sort of poetic justice, allows the Micawbers their fantastic wish-Mr. Micawber does become a magistrate at the very end.

## CHAPTER 37: A LITTLE COLD WATER

Peggotty returns to Yarmouth, leaving Betsey Trotwood to take care of David's chambers. The formidable Mrs. Crupp is utterly defeated by Betsey, and David's rooms soon become more habitable under her housekeeping.

David up to now had never told Dora of his change in fortune, merely hinting at it in his letters. Now that a new rendezvous has been arranged for them at Miss Mills' house, he resolves to tell her all. Abruptly he asks her if she could love a beggar. "How can you ask me anything so foolish? Love a beggar?" she pouts. She refuses to believe he is serious, finally breaking down in tears when he insists he is poor. "Don't talk about being poor, and working hard!" she pleads. He soothes her by picturing their frugal future home, with Jip still enjoying his daily mutton-chop.

David then suggests to Dora that she could prepare for her role as a frugal wife by looking after her father's housekeeping and by learning a bit about accounts. When he adds that he will send her a cook book to study, it is all over. First she sobs, and then she faints. He is vainly trying to revive her when Miss Mills returns. He explains to her what has happened and Miss Mills is both understanding and sympathetic. But she warns David, "Our dearest Dora is a favorite child of nature. She is a thing of light, and airiness, and joy." The accounts, the housekeeping, and cookery, are not for Dora. David takes the warning lightly. He loves her, "most absorbingly, entirely, and completely." That is enough.

## Comment

This silly-tearful encounter between David and Dora allows even the most obtuse reader to realize that she is not the right wife for a struggling young man without money or prospects. That Agnes Wickfield, whom David thinks of only as a "sister," would make a better wife is also rather obvious.

## CHAPTER 38: A DISSOLUTION OF PARTNERSHIP

David plunges resolutely into his plan of learning to take shorthand so as to become a parliamentary reporter. He finds the mastering of the mysterious squiggles, dots, and marks an exceedingly difficult task, almost heartbreaking, but the thought of Dora drives him on. For practice he has Traddles read the speeches of politicians aloud while he attempts to write them down.

One morning when he goes to Doctors' Commons, Mr. Spenlow, instead of returning his greeting, asks him coldly to go with him to a coffee-house close by. In an upstairs room he faces Miss Murdstone, who has discovered his meeting with Dora and has all his letters. The dog, Jip, who was caught carrying one of the letters in his mouth, was the innocent betrayer. Mr. Spenlow is furious, although David vows he loves Dora and wants to marry her. Her father tells David that an engagement is out of the question. "Have you considered my daughter's station in life, the projects I may contemplate for her advancement, the testamentary intentions I may have with reference to her?" He is a man of property and wealth, continues Mr. Spenlow, and he will not allow his well-laid plans for the future to be affected by "youthful folly." "Let there be an end of the nonsense," he concludes.

Completely downstruck, David goes to Miss Mills. That young lady, enjoying her role of confidante to the now separated young lovers, can offer little hope. He confides all to his aunt as well, but she, too, cannot console him, and he goes to bed despairing.

The next morning, when David arrives at the office of Spenlow and Jorkins, he is told the astounding news that Mr.

Spenlow has died the day before. Furthermore, the checking of Mr. Spenlow's desk, in which task David is asked to help by Mr. Jorkins, reveals that Mr. Spenlow has left no will. In fact, after that gentleman's affairs are settled, he is shown to have lived beyond his means, leaving little for Dora. The bereaved girl is sent to live with her two maiden aunts, the Misses Lavinia and Clarissa Spenlow.

## Comment

In this chapter Dickens in the guise of David Copperfield is living again in memory his early romance with Maria Beadnell. His slavery to the mastering of shorthand is true. But the confrontation and rejection by his beloved's father never really happened. Mr. Beadnell, a banker, did not approve of his daughter's getting serious with an impecunious shorthand reporter; to break up the incipient romance he sent Maria off to Paris. Dickens revenges himself by having his fictional counterpart suddenly dying, thus leaving the coast clear for the lovers. Mr. Beadnell did no such obliging thing.

## CHAPTER 39: WICKFIELD AND HEEP

In order to help David overcome his dejection, Aunt Betsey sends him to Dover for a few days to make arrangements for the renting of her old cottage. Neither Doctor Strong, who is glad to see him get a little vacation, nor Mr. Jorkins, whose business is rapidly going downhill, put up any objection.

When the Dover affairs have been looked after, David goes to Canterbury, and he enjoys walking the familiar streets. At Mr. Wickfield's house he finds Mr. Micawber "playing his pen with great assiduity" in the place where Uriah used to sit. Mr. Micawber is quite satisfied with his job, and praises Uriah Heep for being so generous in advancing him money. He refuses to discuss anything of the affairs of Wickfield and Heep. Being employed "in a capacity of confidence," there are topics he cannot discuss even with Mrs. Micawber. David "saw an uneasy change in Mr. Micawber ... as if his new duties were a misfit."

## Comment

Mr. Micawber, although a bad credit risk, is not a criminal type. Here Dickens is scaring the reader into fearing that jolly Micawber is succumbing to the evil wiles of Heep and getting involved in his nefarious schemes.

David also sees Agnes. He tells her how much he misses her calm counsel and support. "When I have come to you," he says, "I have come to peace and happiness. I come home now, like a tired traveller, and find such a blessed sense of rest." He tells her about his troubles concerning Dora, and he finds Agnes sympathetic. She suggests that David write to Dora's new guardians, her aunts, the Misses Spenlow, and lay his cards on the table.

Downstairs, David visits Mr. Wickfield and Uriah. Mrs. Heep is also hovering about, and David is reminded of "two great bats hanging over the whole house, and darkening it with their ugly forms." he is never given a chance to talk to either Agnes or her father. When he goes out to take a walk Uriah follows him. In the course of conversation they exchange some reluctant confidences. David tells Uriah that he is engaged to another and that he need fear no intentions toward Agnes. Heep in turn tells David about his early life. His parents and he were all brought up in charity schools. "They taught us all a deal of umbleness -

not much else that I know of, from morning to night," he says. They were taught to bow and scrape to their "betters." His father had taught him that to be 'umble' was the road to success. "I am very umble to the present moment, Master Copperfield, but I've got a little power!" he adds ominously.

## Comment

Dickens, as David, observes here that it then occurred to him that "this despicable cant of false humility" was not just a Heep characteristic. It was bred into the charity-school children, turning them into fawning hypocrites who hated the society that had formed them.

Later at dinner, David observes Uriah enticing Mr. Wickfield to drink and gloating over his victim. Uriah overreaches himself when he suggests that he might marry Agnes. Mr. Wickfield is almost insane with mingled shame and fury at Heep's insolence and David has a hard task to calm him. Then Mr. Wickfield, now a broken old man, tells David that his morbid grief for his dead wife had started it all. When Agnes comes in to comfort her father, David has her promise that she would never give in to Uriah through a mistaken sense of duty.

Uriah, however, has the last word. He realizes that he has gone too far, and he temporarily retreats. But, as he tells David, he can wait until the ripened pear is ready to fall into his hands.

## CHAPTER 40: THE WANDERER

One night about a week later, David is walking home from Dr. Strong's house. Passing St. Martin's Church, he glimpses a woman who seems vaguely familiar. Before he has had time to search his memory, he sees the well-remembered form of Mr. Peggotty sitting on the church steps. This sight recalls the identity of the woman to him; it is Martha Endell, "the fallen girl," whom Em'ly had helped with the gift of money in Peggotty's kitchen.

David takes Mr. Peggotty to a nearby inn to listen to his story of his search for Em'ly. Mr. Peggotty, he observed, "was greyer, the lines of his face and forehead were deeper, and he had every appearance of having toiled and wandered through all varieties of weather." Mr. Peggotty tells David that he has travelled far but has heard little of the pair. He has traced Em'ly and Steerforth through France to the Mediterranean, to Italy, then to the mountains of Switzerland. Walking as he did, and only occasionally given a ride by kind people, he was unable to catch up with them. After losing trace of them, he has returned to England. At the old houseboat, with its light shining in the window for Em'ly's return, he found some letters. In them, Em'ly poured out her remorse for her deed and begged Ham's forgiveness for what she had done to him. The letters contain money, but because it is from Steerforth, Mr. Peggotty will not use it. "I'd go ten thousand mile," he says, "I'd go till I dropped dead, to lay that money down afore him. If I'd do that, and find my Em'ly, I'm content." Mr. Peggotty tells David that Em'ly and Steerforth are now on the Upper Rhine and he is off tomorrow to find them. David bids him godspeed on his journey. All this while the inn door has been ajar and an eavesdropper has been listening to the news about Em'ly. It was Martha Endell.

## Comment

With this chapter Dickens ended one monthly installment of the novel. It is a good example of his serial technique. What he has done here is to stimulate suspense by re-introducing the Little Em'ly-Steerforth plot, momentarily dropping David's own life story. In a book whose parts took almost two years to read in the order they appeared, the writer must allow the characters of the subplots to surface from time to time, or the reader will have forgotten them. This necessary technique, however, is also a weakness in the novel. It requires improbable coincidences, such as the appearance of Martha Endell, Mr. Peggotty, and David at the same church at the same time. A worse coincidence is yet to come when it is Martha who finds Em'ly, thus saving her from a fate like her own.

## CHAPTER 41: DORA'S AUNTS

At last David receives an answer to his letter to Dora's aunts. The ladies inform him that he may call upon them, bringing a "confidential friend," in order to discuss the subject. With Traddles, David journeys to Putney for the fearful encounter. On the way, Traddles recounts the tale of his own engagement. When he had broached the subject to the family of his Sophy, her mother screamed and fainted and her nine sisters made him feel like a criminal. "You see, Sophy being so much use in the family, none of them could endure the thought of her ever being married," he explains. They are now reconciled because his prospects of making Sophy his bride are so remote. This story does nothing to reassure David of the reception he is going to get from Dora's aunts.

Fortified by a glass of ale from a neighboring tavern, David and Traddles enter the abode of the Misses Spenlow, "two dry little elderly ladies, dressed in black, and each looking wonderfully like a preparation in chip or tan of the late Mr. Spenlow." Clarissa and Lavinia Spenlow in their bird-like manner tell him that the death of their brother has changed the position of Dora, and that he, "a young gentleman possessed of good qualities and honorable character "might pay his respects. They wish to observe the genuineness of his affection for Dora, which both David and Traddles strongly avow. He may visit her twice a week for tea and on Sundays for dinner, but is to have no secret communication with her. David is ecstatic at these reasonable terms.

At last he sees his lovely Dora again. "How beautiful she was in her black frock...," he recalls, "and what a state of bliss I was in...."

Betsey Trotwood soon calls on Dora's aunts and soon becomes intimate with them, although they regard her as "an eccentric and somewhat masculine lady, with a strong understanding." Aunt Betsey joins the Misses Spenlow in treating Dora like a pretty toy, a little child rather than as a young lady soon to be married. "Little Blossom," as Aunt Betsey calls Dora, rather than resenting this treatment, seems to thrive on it.

David renews his attempts to interest Dora in domestic pursuits by buying her a cook book, tablets, and a pretty pencil case to keep accounts with. "But the Cookery Book made Dora's head ache, and the figures made her cry," he reports. All attempts to get her to think seriously about housekeeping are futile, but her refusals are made "in such a charming manner that she was more delightful than ever." Eventually David finds himself treating her like a plaything too.

## Comment

The path is now open for David's marriage to Dora. Again Dickens hints that she is not the right kind of a wife for David, although she is utterly adorable in her own way.

# DAVID COPPERFIELD

........................................................................

### CHAPTER 42: MISCHIEF

It was in teaching himself shorthand, David writes, that he developed the spirit of perseverance, the habits of punctuality and diligence which led to his future success. "Never to put one hand to anything, on which I could throw my whole self; and never to affect depreciation of my work, whatever it was; I find now, to have been my golden rules."

### Comment

In this passage, Dickens drops the mask of David, and announces the philosophy of unremitting toil that enabled a man of his humbled station and poor education to rise to eminence.

Mr. Wickfield and Agnes come to London on a two-week visit to Dr. Strong. David is not surprised to find Mrs. Heep hovering about also. Uriah too is there and he soon collars David in the garden. He hints that jealousy prompts him to keep an eye on Agnes, not of David, but of Jack Maldon, "a lady's man," and of Annie Strong, whose influence he fears. He succeeds in rekindling in David the old suspicions about Jack Maldon and Mrs. Strong. He displays a venomous malice toward Mrs. Strong, born of the snubbing he had endured when he was but a lowly clerk and had not been invited to her home. Toward Jack Maldon he also harbors resentment, for that "fine gentleman ... never could come into the office, without ordering or shoving" him around.

A few evenings later, in fear and trepidation David brings Agnes to meet Dora at her aunts'. He is anxious that Agnes like Dora and he fears that Dora would resent Agnes as "too clever." He is relieved when the girls take an instant liking to each other. Now that Miss Mills has gone to India with her father, Dora needs a new confidante. Dora, in a serious mood later, asks "Doady," as she calls David, "Don't you think, if I had had her for a friend a long time ago,... I might have been more clever perhaps?... I wonder why you ever fell in love with me?" On the way home Agnes praises Dora to David and he feels she is as much Dora's good angel as his. "I can be happier in nothing than in your happiness," she tells David.

## Comment

In bringing Agnes and Dora together, Dickens is preparing us for the final act of this strange romance; Dora when dying tells Agnes to marry her husband, David, after her death. Agnes is, of course, in love with David all this time, but he regards her only as his "sister."

David returns to Dr. Strong's house only to find the doctor in his study with Mr. Wickfield and Uriah. The villain is telling Dr. Strong "that Mr. Maldon, and the lovely and agreeable lady as is Doctor Strong's wife, are too sweet on one another," and that their intrigue has been going on since before Maldon went to India. Both Mr. Wickfield and David are called on as witnesses to these insinuations. The kind doctor does not blame his wife but himself for having married so young a girl. He can hardly blame her for her interest in a man her age, and his faith in her remains strong. He asks them to keep this disclosure a secret. When later Uriah Heep gloats over his move, David strikes him on the face with full force.

## Comment

The Strong triangle sub-plot has reached its **climax**. A real extra-marital affair would not have pleased the Victorian reader, so it will turn out later that Annie Strong is innocent. Meantime, Uriah Heep has been shown to be a more thorough villain, cruel and vindictive, than before.

David notices weeks later that Dr. Strong's conduct toward his wife has changed. He treats her with gentle compassion and urges her to spend more time with her mother, Mrs. Markleham, in an endless round of amusements. Annie feels hurt by her husband's keeping himself apart from her. Into this domestic unhappiness, Mr. Dick, a friend since Canterbury days, enters like a good spirit, walking for hours with the doctor or helping Mrs. Strong in the garden.

Another marriage on the verge of dissolution seems to be that of the Micawbers. David receives a letter from Mrs. Micawber telling him that her husband has changed. He is secretive, morose, severe, estranged from the children and has no pride in the twins. This is clearly not the Micawber of old, David thinks, but he can offer no advice but patience and kindness.

## CHAPTER 43: ANOTHER RETROSPECT

David looks back from the distance of time to this next period of his life. He is now 21, has mastered the intricacies of shorthand, and has become a reporter for a morning newspaper. He has attained a high repute for his accomplishments in reporting the debates in Parliament, but even better, he has branched out to do writing for magazines. His income is good, and he has rented a pleasant little cottage. His aunt is moving to a cottage of her own because David is to be married.

At last the day approaches. For weeks Dora has been fitted for her wedding finery, and has inspected (without much interest) household furnishings. Peggotty has scrubbed and waxed the new cottage to a high gloss. The license is bought, duly filled in with the names of David Copperfield and Dora Spenlow, and there is even the blessing of the Archbishop of Canterbury on it. Traddles' Sophy arrives (she is going to be a bridesmaid) and David finds her "one of the most genial, unaffected, frank,engaging creatures" he has ever met. Agnes Wickfield, another bridesmaid, also comes.

Of the wedding itself, David can recall little, he was in such a daze. It is all a dream to him, walking down the aisle with Dora on his arm, "through a mist of people," of a breakfast and speeches, of himself and Dora at last off in their carriage with Jip, her dog. "Are you happy now, you foolish boy?" asks Dora, "and sure you don't repent it?" They are married and he can hardly believe it.

## Comment

Everybody loves a wedding, and this chapter gave much pleasure to Dickens' readers. The early part of the chapter, which relates his parliamentary reporting and magazine writing, is, of course, autobiographical.

## CHAPTER 44: OUR HOUSEKEEPING

After the honeymoon is over, David still cannot get used to having Dora always there with him. "All the romance of our engagement," he writes, was "put away upon a shelf to rust-no one to please but one another-one another to please, for life."

"I doubt whether two young birds could have known less about keeping house, then I and my pretty Dora did," he says. Their servant, Mary Anne Paragon, belies her name, never has the meals ready on time, can't cook them properly, and causes spoons to disappear. When David asks Dora to reprimand her, she (Dora) breaks into tears because she thinks her housekeeping is being criticized.

## Comment

Dora as an incompetent housewife is no longer a portrait of Maria Beadnell, but of Dickens' wife, Kate Hogarth. Dora, after marriage, takes on more and more of the attributes of the real Mrs. Dickens.

David asks Aunt Betsey to speak to Dora about the housekeeping, but she wisely refuses to meddle. "You have chosen freely for yourself," she admonishes David, "and you have chosen a very pretty and affectionate creature." She tells David that he must accept Dora as she is, and hope to develop qualities in her that she does not have. "No one can assist you; you are to work it out for yourselves. This is marriage, Trot; and Heaven bless you both in it, for a pair of babes in the wood as you are!"

Domestic life goes on in a series of **catastrophes** and fiascos. One incompetent servant succeeds another. The merchants cheat them with shoddy goods and exorbitant prices. Then there is dinner with Traddles as guest. Everything goes wrong: the room is so crowded Traddles can hardly wield knife and fork; Jip walks about on the table, putting his paws into the food and barking continuously; the leg of mutton is almost raw and the oysters (Dora bought a whole barrel) are not even open and they have no tools to open them with.

After the guest has left, Dora tells David that she is sorry, and she wishes he would teach her. She wants him to call her his "child-wife" and to remember that she loves him very much. She makes another attempt, just as futile as the first, to learn to keep household accounts. But she just cannot do it, and David writes that "soon I took upon myself the toils and cares of our life, and had no partner in them." "I did feel, sometimes, for a little while, that I could have wished my wife had been my counsellor, had had more character and purpose, to sustain me, and improve me by; had been endowed with power to fill up the void which sometimes seemed to be about me ... ," he plaintively adds.

David now spends more time writing, for he "was beginning in a small way to be known as a writer," and Dora pleads to be allowed to "help" him by sitting beside him holding his pens.

## Comment

The intimations grow stronger that Dora is not the proper wife for David, the budding young writer. Is this Dickens going through a sour-grapes routine, subconsciously telling himself that marriage with Maria Beadnell would not have worked out anyway?

## CHAPTER 45: MR. DICK FULFILLS MY AUNT'S PREDICTIONS

Meanwhile, in Doctor Strong's house, the relationship between the good doctor and his wife is still strained. Mrs. Markleham, "the Old Soldier" as she is called even by Aunt Betsey, was enjoying herself immensely. The doctor's desire that Annie should have frequent diversion was just what the mother needed as an excuse to take her daughter on an endless round of amusements. Although Annie protests that she is weary, her mother insists that she should make "a proper return for the kindness of Doctor Strong" by going. Mrs. Markleham is really selfishly exploiting the situation.

Mr. Dick, in his simple-minded way, is on the best of terms with both the doctor and his wife. One day he comes to David perplexed over the strain between his two friends, and David explains to him that the doctor and Annie love each other, but cannot get together in reconciliation because of the cloud between them. "I'll bring them together, boy," says Mr. Dick.

One evening and Aunt Betsey stroll over to Dr. Strong's. Mrs. Markleham tells them and Annie that she came into the study to find the doctor there with some lawyers, making his will leaving everything unconditionally to Annie. The "Old Soldier" exults over this, saying that this "suitable provision" is what she always wanted for her daughter from the start.

They go into the study, led by Mr. Dick, and the storm breaks. Annie falls at the doctor's feet, imploring him, "Oh my husband and father, break this long silence. Let us both know what it is that has come between us." She implores those present to speak up and give the reason. David recounts, with some hesitation, the suspicious insinuations of the Uriah Heep about Jack Maldon. Annie admits that before she met the doctor she had loved Jack Maldon, but that her marriage had saved her "from the first mistaken impulse" of her "undisciplined heart." She also realizes that her mother has traded on her marriage to exploit the generosity of her husband, including taking care of Jack Maldon. Annie and the doctor are left reconciled in each other's arms and Mrs. Markleham, who has been fuming and sputtering all this time, has been routed. It was Mr. Dick who had brought this all about in his simple-minded, direct fashion.

"It's very much to be wished that some mothers would leave their daughters alone after marriage," says Aunt Betsey drily to David. But David is thinking of two disturbing things said by Annie to her husband: "There can be no disparity in marriage like unsuitability of mind and purpose" and "the first mistaken impulse of an undisciplined heart." Do they apply to him?

## Comment

The sub-plot of the Strongs is now finished. Critics such as Bruce McCullough (see bibliography) have pointed out that the scene of reconciliation is badly overdone "by the presence of the spectators and the declamatory manner of the wife." Annie sees in the doctor a blend of husband and father, and "it is characteristic of Dickensian optimism that it should take a hopeful view of this marriage between an elderly man and a young woman."

## CHAPTER 46: INTELLIGENCE

About a year of married life has passed for David and Dora. He has grown more successful as a writer by steady application and even now he is taking a walk, thinking about the first novel he is writing. Passing by the Steerforth house, which is not far from his own, he is seen by Rosa Dartle, who invites him in. It develops that she has often seen him passing by and has waited for this opportunity to talk to him.

David finds her little changed from the last time he saw her except that she is thinner, more colorless and her eyes more flashing. Rosa Dartle, he quickly discovers, has called him in to tell him about Steerforth and Em'ly. They have separated, or at least Em'ly has run away from Steerforth; Rosa hopes that she is dead. David is wondering how she has received this news, when Rosa "looking like a cruel princess in a legend" produces her witness, the "ever respectable" Littimer, Steerforth's manservant.

Littimer recounts the travels of Steerforth and Em'ly on the continent. "The young woman," he says, "was very improvable, and spoke the languages, and wouldn't have been known as the same country person.

I notice that she was much admired wherever we went." Em'ly had become to all appearances a "lady," ever her wish. But, continues Littimer, her spirits became low and she began to weary Steerforth, who became restless. One day, from a seaside villa near Naples, Steerforth left for a sailing trip (really to desert her), leaving behind instructions that she "should marry a very respectable person ... who was as good as anybody the young woman could have aspired to" (meaning Littimer).

When Em'ly was told this, she almost went mad and had to be confined to prevent murder or suicide. Littimer thinks her conduct ungrateful, outrageous, and unreasonable. One day she managed to escape through a window, and she has disappeared.

## Comment

This callous tossing aside of the poor but sweet maiden by the spoiled, rich seducer is according to the rules of melodrama. All this came about, the implication reads, because Em'ly wanted to become a "lady," rather than a fisherman's wife.

After Littimer has been dismissed, Rosa and David are joined by Mrs. Steerforth. She is greatly altered, David notes, "her fine figure was far less upright, her handsome face was deeply marked, and her hair was almost white." She tells David that although she has heard from Steerforth he has not regained "his sense of duty or natural obligation." She is happy to hear that David is married and even becoming a little famous. It is a pity, she adds, that his mother is dead, for she would have been so proud of him.

David visits Mr. Peggotty at his humble lodgings to tell him what he has learned. They decide that Em'ly, who Mr. Peggotty feels certain to be alive, would come to London to lose herself amidst the crowds. They also think that Martha Endell, who knows the seamy side of the city, could help them find Em'ly. Before they go out, David sees Mr. Peggotty lay out one of Em'ly's dresses and a bonnet upon her return. After some wandering in the nighttime streets, they spy the solitary figure of Martha and follow it.

## Comment

This chapter is another digression from David Copperfield's own life story. It came at the end of a monthly installment of the novel, and by stirring up renewed interest in the Steerforth-Em'ly subplot Dickens stimulates the desire to read the next installment.

## CHAPTER 47: MARTHA

On the edge of the river, David and Mr. Peggotty at last catch up with Martha. When they approach her and she recognizes them, she dissolves into a flood of tears. "Oh, the river!" she cried, "I know that I belong to it. I know that it's the natural company of such as I am! It comes from country places, where there was once no harm in it - and it creeps through the dismal streets, defiled and miserable - and it goes away, like my life, to a great sea, that is always troubled - and I feel that I must go with it!"

## Comment

In the description of the dismal riverside of London, Dickens is magnificent, but his pathos is again overpowering. Martha's self-abasement seems somewhat extreme to us today.

"I am bad, I am lost. I have no hope at all," Martha continues. But, she says, she will do everything in her power to help them find Em'ly and thus preserve her from a fate like hers. All she asks is that they trust her and she refuses to take any money.

Later that night, on his way home, David sees a light still lit in his aunt's cottage. Upon investigation, he sees that a man is standing in the garden, the same man whom he had once thought to be a delusion of Mr. Dick's. Keeping himself from view, David sees his aunt give the man money and tell him that it is all she has. Grumbling, the man leaves.

After Aunt Betsey has calmed herself, she tells David about the man. He is her husband from whom long ago she had separated. He had treated her shamefully, had spent most of her money, and although she knew he was an adventurer and gambler, she had given him additional sums of money from time to time to keep him from utter destitution. "I was a fool when I married him," she admits. For the sake of what he once had been to her she is still "an incurable fool on the subject." She admonishes David to keep the story to himself.

## Comment

The revelation of the identity of the stranger is hardly a surprise. But it serves to make the formidable Betsey Trotwood more human to find that she is capable of sentimental attachments and has made a wrong marriage.

## CHAPTER 48: DOMESTIC

By hard work, and without letting his writing interfere with his newspaper duties, David completes his book. Published, it is a great success, but David remains modest. "The more praise I got," he writes, "the more I tried to deserve." He feels "that nature and accident" have "made him an author" and he gives up parliamentary reporting to devote himself to his new profession.

The time is now a year and a half since his marriage. He and Dora have given up all attempts at housekeeping. "The house kept itself and we kept a page," he writes. The page fights with the cook, drinks their wine, steals and sells their food, and finally is jailed for stealing Dora's gold watch. This dismal even leads David to remonstrate with Dora over their poor housekeeping. Their laxity, he says, is infecting all who come in contact with them. Dora, of course, takes this as a personal rebuke and commences weeping.

## Comment

By now, Dora, as the helpless, incompetent housewife, has lost all traces of Maria Beadnell and has become even more like Kate, Dickens' real-life wife.

He determines to "form Dora's mind" by reading Shakespeare to her, and giving her "little scraps of useful information; or sound opinion." It is futile, for Dora's mind was as "formed" as it ever would be, her realizes. He resolves to accept her as she is, and goes back to treating her like a child wife. But he is vaguely unhappy, thinking "it would have been better for me if my wife could have helped me more, and shared the many thoughts in which I had no partner." Sometimes in this mood he thinks of the contented days with Agnes and he wonders what would have happened if he had never met Dora. Two phrases keep haunting him: "the first mistaken impulse of an undisciplined heart" and "no disparity in marriage like unsuitability of mind and purpose." He tries hard to adapt himself to Dora.

He hopes that a baby will change his child wife to a woman, but the baby dies at birth. Dora does not seem to recover her strength, and he has to carry her up and down the stairs. Dora worries only that Jip is getting slow and lazy, but Aunt Betsey, who is nursing Dora, points out that the dog is getting old.

Weeks pass and Dora remains an invalid. David, when he carries her upstairs in the evening, can feel her getting lighter and lighter. The "Little Blossom," as his aunt calls her, has withered fast, he reflects sadly.

## Comment

Dickens is preparing the reader for the death of Dora. David's vague dissatisfaction with Dora's mind, not capable of being "formed" and providing no intellectual companionship for him, makes it almost necessary. Only death, in Victorian England, could make it possible to marry again, this time to the "right" wife for a successful writer. Charles Dickens in real life had no such luck.

## CHAPTER 49: I AM INVOLVED IN MYSTERY

One day David receives a mystifying letter from Mr. Micawber. Puzzling his way through the tortuous rhetorical flourishes, he understands that he and Traddles are to meet Micawber outside the King's Bench Prison the day after tomorrow at seven o'clock in the evening. David decides that something important lies hidden in this letter. When Traddles joins him he finds that his friend has also received a mysterious missive, but from Mr. Micawber. She writes that her husband's conduct has become unbearable; he has even threatened he twins with an oyster knife! He is going to London, and she hopes they can meet him and find out what has caused this horrible change.

When the appointed time comes, David and Traddles meet Micawber. In the shadow of the prison he tells them that he was better off in the days when he was a prisoner inside. At least he could look his fellow-man in the face. When they query him for the reason for his depression, he grows evasive, especially in regard to the merest mention of his employer, Heep. They invite him to Aunt Betsey's house to make a bowl of his famous punch. The thought of this brightens him immediately.

The kind attentions of Aunt Betsey, Mr. Dick, Traddles, and David thaw out Mr. Micawber by degrees. He fumbles at making the punch, "putting the lemon peel into the kettle, the sugar into the snuffer-tray, the spirit into the empty jug." When David asks him what is the matter, he replies, "Villainy is the matter; baseness is the matter; deception, fraud, conspiracy, are the matter; and the name of the whole atrocious mass is-Heep!" In a week from today, he continues, they are all to meet for breakfast in the inn at Canterbury. There he will effect "redress from wrongs inflicted by consummate scoundrel-Heep."

## Comment

Like a juggler catching the tossed-up oranges one by one, Dickens is gathering in his subplots. The Wickfield-Heep affair is now about to be wound up.

# DAVID COPPERFIELD

## CHAPTERS 50-64

. . . . . . . . . . . . . . . . . . . . . . . . . . . . . . . . . . . . . . . . . . . . . . . . .

### CHAPTER 50: MR. PEGGOTTY'S DREAM COMES TRUE

Months pass and David neither sees Martha again nor hears of any news of Em'ly. David begins to despair that Em'ly must be dead, but Mr. Peggotty retains the certain conviction that she is alive and will be found. David's admiration for the rugged old man increases as he observes his selfless devotion to the search.

One evening Martha comes to David and asks him to go with her. She has left a note with the address in Mr. Peggotty's room in order that he too could join them on his return. They take a coach into London, where Martha leads David to a decaying old mansion, now a lodging house, in which she lives. As they climb the rickety stairs they see a female figure up ahead of them. They arrive at the top floor just in time to see this person enter Martha's rooms. David recognizes her as Rosa Dartle. Martha leads him into her room by another entrance and he can listen to the dialogue between Rosa and another woman inside. He recognizes the voice as that of Em'ly.

---

## Comment

Several scholars have noted that Dickens frequently has David in the position of eavesdropping on private scenes like this. Generally in the latter part of the novel, David is more an observer of the crises in the lives of other people (the Strongs, the Micawbers, the Trotwoods, the Peggottys) than a participant in events.

"I have come," he hears Rosa say, "to see James Steerforth's fancy; ... I want to know what such a thing is like." David shudders at "the resolute and unrelenting hatred of her tone, its cold stern sharpness and its mastered rage...." But he does not want to interfere or make his presence known, because he feels that Mr. Peggotty should see Em'ly first.

The scene that passes between the vindictive Rosa and the cringing Em'ly is harrowing in the extreme. Rosa calls her a "purchased slave" who should reserve her "false arts" for her "dupes." That Em'ly has disgraced her own home is nothing to her. "You were a part of the trade of your home and were bought and sold like any other vendible thing your people dealt in," she says. That she has been the "cause of division between lady-mother and gentleman-son; of grief in a house where she wouldn't have been admitted as a kitchen-girl ..." is the evil. "If I could order it to be done, I would have this girl whipped to death," she adds.

She tells the almost senseless Em'ly that if she doesn't either disappear completely or kill herself, she will see to it that she is persecuted. Just then, footsteps are heard coming up the stairs.

Rosa glides out as Mr. Peggotty comes in. With the fearful cry of "Uncle," she greets him and faints. He picks up the unconscious Em'ly and carries her down the stairs.

## Comment

The Em'ly-Steerforth plot has reached a **climax** in this chapter which ended a monthly installment of the novel. The dialogue between Rosa and Em'ly, like that between Dr. Strong and Annie, strikes us as overdone. It is hard to believe that people, even in Victorian England, ever talked like this.

## CHAPTER 51: THE BEGINNINGS OF A LONGER JOURNEY

Early the next morning, Mr. Peggotty comes to David to relate the story of Em'ly's wanderings as she had told it to him. It seems that when she had escaped from the house near Naples where Littimer had kept her after Steerforth's desertion, she had run wildly down the beach. Unconscious and exhausted, she had been found by a seaman's wife, an Italian woman she had often spoken to before. This kind person sheltered her in her humble home, and nursed her through a long period of illness in which she was out of her mind with fever. She recovered slowly and when the woman's husband returned from a voyage, they put her on a small ship bound for France. Mr. Peggotty blesses these people for having been so good to Em'ly, although they were poor.

In France, Em'ly had worked at an inn, waiting on travelling ladies, but once seeing Littimer lurking about, she fled across the Channel to England. Afraid and ashamed to return to her old home at Yarmouth, Em'ly went to London. She had just fallen into the clutches of an evil woman, who would have led her to prostitution, when Martha found her. It was Martha, who "brought her safe out, in the dead of night, from that black pit of ruin."

## Comment

Mr. Peggotty's recapitulation of Em'ly's story begins a new monthly installment. This device would be unnecessary in a novel meant to be read continuously.

Mr. Peggotty then tells David that he has decided to leave England. "No one can't reproach my darling in Australia. We will begin a new life over there!" he says. He wants David to return to the Steerforths all the money that had been sent. He also wants David to go to Yarmouth with him to say his farewells and settle his affairs.

The next day David and Mr. Peggotty take the mail coach to Yarmouth. David lingers at Omer and Joram's shop (the undertaker-draper-tailor), to chat with old Mr. Omer, whom he finds in a wheelchair smoking his favorite pipe. Mr. Omer is enjoying old age, content with the prospering business of his son-in-law and his pretty grandchildren. He tells David that he has enjoyed reading his novels and is proud to know such an author.

David continues on to Ham's house, to which Mr. Peggotty has preceded him. He finds Peggotty and Mrs. Gummidge there too, bathed in tears of mingled sorrow and joy. When he gets a chance to talk to Ham alone, David realizes that Ham is suffering from a broken heart. Ham is somehow reproaching himself for Em'ly's fate. Had she not been engaged to him she would have confided the Steerforth affair to him and he might have prevented it, he reasons. He asks David to tell Em'ly that he isn't badly hurt, so that she wouldn't worry.

One more emotion-packed scene ensues when, as the old house boat is being emptied of its furnishings, Mrs. Gummidge begs Mr. Peggotty to take her along to Australia. Although she is a "lone and lorn creature" (her favorite expression), she will follow him anywhere, bearing the rigors of travel and hardship. Mr. Peggotty consents, and a happy Mrs. Gummidge accompanies them on the return trip to London.

## Comment

In this chapter Dickens is preparing to clear the decks of the host of minor characters who have cluttered up the novel. Shipping them off to Australia was not just a handy device either. Dickens had great faith in emigration, especially to Australia, as a means of solving many of the social problems of England.

## CHAPTER 52: I ASSIST AT AN EXPLOSION

The time has come at which they are to meet Mr. Micawber at the Canterbury inn for the mysterious disclosures about Heep. Aunt Betsey goes along too, urged by Dora, who insists she is not ill enough to need constant nursing. Punctually at half-past nine, Mr. Micawber appears to join David, Traddles, Aunt Betsey and Mr. Dick, who are awaiting him. He tells them that he and Traddles have been in consultation about this matter for some time. Five minutes after he leaves, they are to follow him to the Wickfield-Heep house for the revelation.

When they arrive, Mr. Micawber ushers them into the presence of Uriah Heep, who feigns pleasure at the visit. His mood turns to one of anxious surprise when Mr. Micawber defiantly refuses to leave the room. Instead Mr. Micawber denounces Heep as a scoundrel. Heep grows ugly at the realization that this meeting is a "conspiracy." "You were always a puppy with a proud stomach ... ," he sneers at David, "and you envy me my rise, do you?" He threatens each in turn: Micawber with his debts, Aunt Betsey with her husband (how he knows him we are never informed), Agnes with her father's ruin.

As Micawber reads off a prepared statement (full of his usual grand language) on the illegal misdeeds of Heep, Uriah drops his mask of humility completely. They all see the hatred, malice, and insolence which really move Heep. Micawber's document reveals that Heep has systematically defrauded Mr. Wickfield, forging his name to documents, misappropriating funds, and making it appear that his employer has done so. The evidence is a notebook, which Heep thought he had burned, but which Micawber has saved from the ashes. Mrs. Heep implores her son to "be umble and make terms," realizing that he has been defeated and is now in danger of prison.

Aunt Betsey seizes Heep by the collar and demands her money. She had never said anything about the lost investment because she thought that Mr. Wickfield had embezzled it. When Traddles asks David to get the police, Heep surrenders. He is to relinquish all the documents which have given him a hold over the Wickfields and make complete restitution.

## Comment

In this grand scene, the Wickfield-Heep plot comes to a **climax** in the thwarting of the villainous Heep. By one stroke Agnes is safe from Heep, Mr. Wickfield on the road to rehabilitation, Micawber made a hero and restored to his family, and Aunt Betsey's fortune recovered. That all this hangs upon a very precarious thread - the unburned notebook (which a villain as cunning as Heep would never have left unburned) - seems irrelevant.

David sees Mr. Micawber reunited with his long-suffering wife Emma and their numerous progeny. After the emotional storm has subsided, the Micawbers reflect on the bleak future. Aunt Betsey brightly suggests that the Micawbers join the Peggottys in migrating to Australia. After ascertaining that the climate is good, the opportunities for a man of Micawber's talents great, and that Aunt Betsey will pay for the trip, they agree.

## CHAPTER 53: ANOTHER RETROSPECT

David, writing his memories, looks back on this sad period of his life, the day of Dora's death. As weeks and then months go by and Dora gets no better, he begins to fear that she will never recover. He will never see his "child-wife running in the sunlight with her old friend, Jip," who has grown very old. The dog is feeble and almost blind now.

One day Dora asks David to send for Agnes. She wants to know if he is very lonely without her downstairs, for she is now bedridden. She expresses the notion that she will never be well again. David tries to comfort her, but he knows now that she is not long for this world.

During their last time together, Dora tells David that she realizes she was not fit to be his wife. "I am afraid, dear," she says softly, "I was too young. I don't mean in years only, but in experience, and thoughts, and everything." They have been happy, she admits, but in time he "would have wearied of his child-wife." David begs her through his tears not to reproach herself so. He notices too that she refers to herself in the past tense, as though already dead. Finally she asks David to send Agnes up, for she wishes to speak to her alone. "It is much better as it is," are her parting words to David.

David sends Agnes upstairs and is left alone with Jip. The old dog crawls over to David, licks his hand, whines to go upstairs, and lies down at his feet where with a cry he expires. Just then Agnes returns and David can see by her face what has happened. Dora is dead.

## Comment

Again Dickens has descended into bathos, but leaving his audience tear-stained in the process. Deathbed scenes like this were always favorites when Dickens gave public readings from his novels. That Jip, the little dog always associated with Dora, should die at the same instant as his mistress, is the crowning touch - the combination of sentimentality with coincidence.

## CHAPTER 54: MR. MICAWBER'S TRANSACTIONS

Gradually David's mind emerges from the dark sea of grief. It was probably Agnes, he recalls now, who suggested that he travel for awhile and thus restore his peace of mind. But first he had to await several pieces of unfinished business, the final settlement of the Heep affair, and the embarkation of the emigrants to Australia.

Micawber and his family are already preparing themselves for their future lives as pioneers in "the Bush." His oldest daughter is learning how to milk cows, the younger children observing the raising of pigs and poultry. But he is fearful that Heep, who holds IOU's in the sum of 103 pounds, will have him jailed for debt. Aunt Betsey orders that whenever this happens. Micawber's debts are to be paid.

Traddles reports on the affairs of the firm of Wickfield, whose accounts he has audited. All the money has been accounted for except two thousand pounds of Aunt Betsey's, but she then admits to having withdrawn it years ago "for a rainy day." She had never said anything because she wanted to see how David would do on his own, thinking her penniless. Mr. Wickfield's business, however, even after the house is old, would have little capital left. Agnes resolves to rent the old house and open up a school. Then she can "render back some little portion of the love and care" she owes her father, and be "useful and happy."

Traddles explains that Heep had embezzled Aunt Betsey's money, not so much out of greed, but out of hatred for David. He and his mother have fled to London and Traddles predicts that his old crookedness will continue.

Traddles inquires discreetly about the threat to Aunt Betsey regarding her husband. This threat disappears one day when she asks David to go to a London hospital with her. A hearse is waiting and in it is the body of her husband. He has died just 36 years to the day after their marriage. "He was a fine-looking man when I married him, Trot," she muses, "and he was sadly changed."

## Comment

With this chapter Dickens began another monthly installment and as usual recapitulates some of the previous month's occurrences. He is also clearing the deck of more of the minor characters.

## CHAPTER 55: TEMPEST

David finds it hard to write of the next event that befell him, "so indelible, so awful, so bound by an infinite variety of ties to all that has preceded it...." To this day he associates it with any stormy wind or mere mention of the seashore.

According to Ham's request, David had written to Em'ly to tell her of Ham's feelings. When he receives an answer from her for Ham, he decides to deliver it to Ham in person. The letter, which Em'ly asked him to read, states that she bids Ham "goodbye forever in this world. In another world, if I am forgiven, I may wake a child and come to you."

## Comment

That Dickens would not allow these unhappy lovers to come together at last strikes us as unduly harsh. However, in Victorian fiction, the "fallen girl," no matter how repentant, cannot marry her "good" lover, no matter how forgiving.

As David rides down to Yarmouth in the evening, he notices that the sky is remarkable, "a colour like the colour of the smoke from damp fuel." The wind increases until the horses can hardly make their way against it. When he arrives at the Yarmouth inn, he sees that the tide flats are covered with water and that the land itself is lashed with sea-spray. Half of the anxious population is on the shore, some just watching the storm, others awaiting the men still at sea. David cannot find Ham and goes back to the inn.

The next morning he is awakened by the news that there is a ship foundering offshore. He goes out to look and sees the vessel, with its crew plainly visible, trying to clear the decks of spars and sails from the broken masts. A huge wave sweeps over the ship, sending most of the men into a watery grave. Four are left until another wave breaks, leaving but two, then another, leaving but one solitary figure clinging to the mast.

At this point, Ham appears and David, distracted by the terrible sights he has seen, asks him if something cannot be done to save the lone survivor. Ham swims out to the wreck with a rope tied to his waist. Just as he is to climb aboard, a huge wave sweeps over the ship and both the lone man and his would-be rescuer are lost. Ham is pulled ashore dead. A little later the body of the man he tried to save is washed ashore. At the very spot where the old Peggotty houseboat, now wrecked, once stood, is James Steerforth, "lying with his head upon his arm," as David had so often seen him at school.

## Comment

While the description of the storm is superb, the deaths of Ham and Steerforth are a web of improbable coincidences. Note, however, how Dickens prepared for this scene as far back as Chapter 21.

## CHAPTER 56: THE NEW WOUND, AND THE OLD

It is David's sad duty to accompany the body of Steerforth to London and to break the news to his mother. He finds Mrs. Steerforth, now an invalid, in her son's former room in which his trophies and mementoes still stand, just as he had left them.

With her is Rosa Dartle, and David sees that she senses that he is the bearer of bad news. Mrs. Steerforth offers condolences on the death of his wife, but when he hints at Steerforth's death, she turns to stone.

It is Rosa Dartle who bursts out into a storm of grief and rage. "Look at me, I say," she cries, "proud mother of a proud false son! Moan for your nurture of him, moan for your corruption of him, moan for your loss of him, moan for mine!"

"I loved him better than you ever loved him," she continues, "If I had been his wife, I could have been the slave of his caprices for a word of love a year." She confesses that she and Steerforth had been lovers, or at least that she had been his plaything until they wearied of each other. David tries to stop this tirade, which it plunging the bereaved mother ever deeper into a coma. Mrs. Steerforth sits there rigidly, moaning all the while. At last Rosa kneels before the pitiful figure and comforts it. David leaves the women to their grief.

## Comment

This scene, powerful as it is, seems overdone in its emotional extravagance. There is poetic justice in that Steerforth's death is the result ultimately of the selfish, corrupt love both women have encouraged in him.

## CHAPTER 57: THE EMIGRANTS

David now sees the emigrants off to Australia. He takes Micawber into his confidence, telling him that he doesn't want Mr. Peggotty or Em'ly to know of the tragedy. Micawber is to intercept newspapers which might tell about the storm and its casualties. David prefers that they leave England "in happy ignorance."

The Micawbers are all prepared for the long voyage, with Mr. Micawber arrayed in a suit of nautical oil-skins and carrying a telescope under his arm. He makes them all a farewell tankard of his famous punch and has to be rescued for the last time from the sheriff for debt. Mrs. Micawber makes a farewell speech in which she outlines the great opportunities awaiting her husband "in a distant country" where "he may be fully understood and appreciated for the first time."

The next day David goes to the wharf to see the ship sail. On board he spies Em'ly standing beside her uncle, waving goodbye to him. He is re-assured, as the ship passes from sight, by the fact that the kind Mr. Peggotty is also taking Martha Endell with him to Australia to start a new life. As night falls, with the leaving of so many of his old friends, he feels it has also fallen darkly upon him.

## Comment

With this chapter Dickens has cleared the stage of the remaining minor characters. Only he and Agnes are left to play out the remainder of the plot.

## CHAPTER 58: ABSENCE

Now that his friends are gone, David, too, leaves England, Little by little his mood grows darker as he realizes the extent of his losses. "I mourned for my child-wife, taken from her blooming world, so young. I mourned for him who might have won the love and admiration of thousands, as he had won mine long ago. I mourned for the broken heart that had found rest in the stormy sea ...," he writes.

For many months he travels with "this ever-darkening cloud" on his mind, he hardly can recall where. At last he settles down in Switzerland where the grandeur of Nature brings relief to his troubled heart. Letters from Agnes, which finally reach him, also help to bring him out of his despondency. She urges him to go back to writing, confident in his power to turn calamity to triumph. He feels the darkness lifting from his soul.

David turns to writing with renewed will, sending the manuscripts to Traddles, who arranges for their publication. His health returns, his reputation as a writer grows, and he begins his third novel. The longing to go home comes over him, for he has been gone almost three years.

One of the flashes of self-revelation that has come to David in this time is that he is in love with Agnes. He thinks that once she must have loved him too, but, he writes, "I had bestowed my passionate tenderness upon another object...." He had insisted on treating Agnes like a sister, and now he cannot expect her to love him as anything but a brother. It was all too late and he "had deservedly lost her." With these bittersweet reflections of what might have been, but could never be, he prepares to return to England.

## Comment

David has come to realize something that the reader knew long before, that Agnes was the right girl for him. The reader is also sure that he will get her (this is the last installment of the novel, and a Victorian novel must end happily). Biographers with a psychological bent have wondered about Agnes. Was she a projection of the ideal wife whom Dickens never knew? She seems too angelic to be real.

## CHAPTER 59: RETURN

On a wintry autumn evening, David lands in London, sometime before his announced return, in order that he can surprise his friends. He first looks up Traddles, who has rooms in Gray's Inn, the legal district where he now has a small practice. As he climbs the stairs to the top story where Traddles lives, David hears peals of girlish laughter. When he is greeted by Traddles, this is explained. Traddles has married his Sophy, one of ten daughters, and not only does she live with him, but so do some of the sisters! Traddles is proud that David has become a famous writer, and David is mightily pleased with the charming Sophy and her pretty sisters. David leaves them, cheered by the atmosphere of the Traddleses domestic bliss.

At a coffee house nearby, he meets old Doctor Chillip, the Blunderstone physician who had helped bring him into the world. The meek little man, after taking awhile to recognize the grown-up David, tells him that the second Mrs. Murdstone has had "her spirit entirely broken" and "is all but melancholy mad." The Murdstones, with their policy of "firmness" have done it again. "… What such people miscall their religion, is a vent for their bad-humours and arrogance," he adds.

On another day, David bursts in upon his Aunt, Mr. Dick, and his old nurse, Peggotty, who are living in the old Trotwood cottage in Dover again.

## Comment

In this chapter Dickens has rounded up more minor plot threads. The long-awaited marriage of his friend Traddles has come off happily. That Dr. Chillip and the Murdstones had to be brought up again seems less necessary. It is also curious that he leaves this monstrous pair unpunished.

## CHAPTER 60: AGNES

David and his aunt have a long talk that night about the many things that have happened in the past three years. Mr. Micawber has actually sent small sums to repay her. Mr. Dick still occupies himself by endless copying of documents, fighting off manfully all references to King Charles I (his mania). She also tells him that Mr. Wickfield, though grown old, "is a reclaimed man," and that Agnes is "as good, as beautiful, as earnest" as ever. He hesitatingly asks if Agnes has a lover. "She might have married twenty times, my dear, since you have gone," is the reply. Agnes seems to have an "attachment," but Aunt Betsey will not tell him more, for it is merely a suspicion on her part, she says.

David rides over to Canterbury to visit Agnes. Looking into her serene eyes, David finds it impossible to tell her what he feels. She tells him of her tranquil life, her little school, but when he tries to lead the conversation to the "attachment," she grows uneasy. David realizes that he must let her broach the subject on her own. "It was for me to guard this sisterly affection with religious care," he writes. "It was all that I had left myself, and it was a treasure."

As he rides home, he knows that neither of them is happy. But the past is dead, and only "in the mystery to come," he "might yet love her with a love unknown on earth...."

## Comment

The suspense of the David-Agnes romance is being built up to a high pitch. By now everybody knows that they love each other, except the parties involved.

## CHAPTER 61: I AM SHOWN TWO INTERESTING PENITENTS

David takes up residence at his Aunt's cottage at Dover while he is completing his newest book. Once in awhile he goes to London to see Traddles, who is taking care of his business affairs. He finds that the amount of mail from his readers has grown heavy, so that he opens an office at the Traddleses place from which it can be answered.

Traddles surprises him by announcing that not only is his Sophy a bright, cheerful housewife, but she has developed a perfect legal hand and is functioning as his copying clerk as well. David envies Traddles and Sophy, who though still struggling financially, are so blissfully happy.

One day, among the letters for David is one from Mr. Creakle, the ferocious schoolmaster of Salem House days so long ago. He is now a magistrate, running what he considers a model prison, and he asks David to inspect it. (Creakle has a much background and competence to be a magistrate as he had had to be a schoolmaster. He got the appointment through politics, not merit, says Traddles.)

Traddles and David go off to inspect this "ideal" prison, a huge building, whose expense, comments David, would have caused an uproar if spent on a school or old-age home.

Mr. Creakle proudly shows them the place, and David notes that the prisoners eat better than most of the working population outside. Creakle explains that the heart of his prison is "the reduction of prisoners to a wholesome state of mind" by solitary confinement. He is especially proud of two prisoners-numbers 27 and 28-whose professions of total reform are proof that his system works. When the cell of Number 27 is opened, David and Traddles see none other before them but Uriah Heep. He brings on a murmur of admiration when he not only is humble enough to recognize his visitors, but forgives David for once striking him. He asks for permission to write his mother so that she too could be brought to his state of true repentance. "It would be better for everybody if they got took up, and was brought here," he says. "There's nothing but sin everywhere-except here."

Prisoner Number 28 is another old acquaintance, the "respectable" Littimer, Steerforth's man-servant. He, too, is a model of reform, but David hears from the warden that he had been convicted of robbing his young master. By a quirk of fate it had been little Miss Mowcher, the dwarf hairdresser, who had caught him just as he was about to flee the country in disguise. David sees that it is vain to argue with Creakle that these repentances are false and hypocritical, and that the system is unworkable.

## Comment

Dickens is still accounting for all the minor characters of earlier chapters, a novelistic device dear to the nineteenth century. More important, he is expressing his views on one of his favorite topics-prisons. In his magazine, *Household Words*,

Dickens had blasted "model" prisons in which prisoners were coddled.

## CHAPTER 62: A LIGHT SHINES ON MY WAY

Christmas is approaching and David still lives with his aunt. Once a week or so he rides over to visit Agnes. He reads to her part of the novel he is writing, and so helpful is her comment that he wishes he had married her instead of Dora; Agnes is all he wishes a wife to be. He still hopes someday to find the right opportunity to tell her of his love.

One day just after Christmas, his aunt tells him that she is now sure Agnes has a definite attachment to someone. What is more, she is going to be married to him. This statement goads David into action. He rides to Canterbury and almost demands to know whom she loves. Agnes won't tell him, except to say that it is not a new attachment. This gives David the hope which spurs him to declare his love for her. She sinks into his arms, telling him that she has loved him all her life.

David and Agnes are married two weeks later. Traddles, Sophy, and Doctor and Mrs. Strong are the only guests at the quiet wedding. Agnes confesses to David that the night Dora died she had made a last request-that Agnes should take her place.

## Comment

Although David and Agnes now have come together at last, the climax leaves us unsatisfied. Agnes might be the Victorian Englishman's dream of the perfect wife, but we might find her angelic sweetness somewhat wearying.

## CHAPTER 63: A VISITOR

David writes that his memoirs are about completed, but "one thread in the web" must still be unraveled. Ten years of life has passed, filled with a happy marriage, numerous children, and ever-growing fame. One night a visitor appears, an old man who looks like a farmer, the servant says. It is Mr. Peggotty, hale and hearty as ever. Over a glass of Yarmouth grog he recounts the adventures of the Australian emigrants. They have prospered in stock farming. Em'ly might have married many times, but never did. Martha Endell has married and is doing well. Even old Mrs. Gummidge could have married, but repulsed the eager suitor. She is no longer "lone and lorn," but a willing and cheerful helper.

The biggest surprise to David is the news of Mr. Micawber. Not only has he paid off all his debts, even those owed to Traddles, but he has prospered. He is now a District Magistrate, and Mr. Peggotty shows David a newspaper clipping with an account of a public dinner tendered him. David reads that the dinner was presided over by Doctor Mell of Colonial Salem House School, the same Mr. Mell who was once a starveling schoolmaster under Creakle.

Before returning to Australia, Mr. Peggotty takes a little earth and a tuft of grass from Ham's grave, "for Em'ly."

## Comment

Mr. Micawber as a magistrate seems rather preposterous, but then Australia for Dickens was the answer to all of England's problems, the land where dreams come true.

## CHAPTER 64: A LAST RETROSPECT

In this last chapter David looks back on his life from a distance of many years. He relates what has become of his many old friends. Aunt Betsey, now over 80 years old, still can walk "six miles at a stretch in winter weather." Peggotty, too, is still vigorous and takes care of his children the way she once did of him. Mr. Dick is teaching his boys to fly kites and hopes to finish his Memorial. Mrs. Steerforth and Rosa Dartle still live together, alternately quarreling and consoling each other in their embittered loneliness. Julia Mills has returned from India, married to a rich old Scotchman, but unhappy. Doctor and Mrs. Strong are happy in their marriage. Traddles is on the way to a judgeship and most of Sophy's sisters have been married off. As David closes the book he thinks of "one face shining on him like a heavenly light" - that on Agnes, who will always guide his life upward.

## Comment

With this final rounding-up, even the most insignificant people are accounted for. The novel, in its ending, seems like a vehicle which has coasted slowly to a stop after its engine was shut off. We realize now that we lost David Copperfield several chapters ago, or else that he has grown up into a stuffy old author.

# DAVID COPPERFIELD

. . . . . . . . . . . . . . . . . . . . . . . . . . . . . . . . . . . . . . . . . . . . . . . . . . . . .

## DAVID COPPERFIELD

As a small boy, he is shown to be affectionate toward his mother and Peggotty, and would probably have been that way to Mr. Murdstone, if allowed to. He is imaginative and sensitive, suffering more from psychic anguish than from physical abuse. Thus he is more horrified by the coldness and mental cruelty of the Murdstones than hurt by the beating he receives. David flourishes and expands under affection, but shrivels and contracts deprived of it. Thus he learns well under his mother's gentle tutoring, but becomes a seeming moron under the harsh task-mastery of the Murdstones.

His youthful character goes through its fire baptism upon the death of his mother. He is taken from the school, allowed to vegetate in neglect at home, and he has fears of "growing up to be a shabby, moody man, lounging an idle life away...." The life in the warehouse, which follows, in worse, for now he loses his hope of "growing up to be a learned and distinguished man."

He survives this ordeal with the moral support of several adults - the Micawbers, Aunt Betsey, and Dr. Strong, who educates him. The second test of his character comes when Aunt Betsey's fortune fails, and he must rely entirely upon himself. He discovers enormous reserves of strength within - a dogged perseverance which enables him to master the difficult art of shorthand reporting. This trait stands him in good stead when he becomes a writer, and is the key to his later success. But he still needs moral support, and his growing disappointment in Dora is that she is unable to help him.

## CLARA COPPERFIELD

David's mother. She is pretty, affectionate, impractical and weak-willed. A young widow, she is easily taken in by the hypocritical Murdstone, who marries her and breaks her spirit, bringing her to an early grave.

## BETSEY TROTWOOD

David's paternal great-aunt. She is formidable, eccentric woman, well-to-do, strong-willed, and with a heart of gold behind her harsh exterior. She is David's fairy godmother, whose money provides for his education.

## CLARA PEGGOTTY

David's nurse and his mother's housekeeper. She is a diamond in the rough, who after his mother's death becomes a substitute mother to him.

## DOCTOR CHILLIP

The meek little physician who brought David into the world and who attends his mother in her last illness.

## EDWARD MURDSTONE

David's step-father. A handsome man but with a streak of cruelty which he disguises as "firmness." He is domineering, taking delight in breaking the spirits of those subject to him. After the death of David's mother, he remarries and treats his new wife the same way.

## JANE MURDSTONE

Edward Murdstone's sister, who is taken into the household after his marriage to David's mother to manage it. As great a believer in "firmness" as her brother. Later, as the chaperone of Dora Spenlow, she almost succeeds in breaking up the romance with David.

## MR. QUINION

Business associate of Mr. Murdstone. At his suggestion David is put to work in the warehouse.

## DANIEL PEGGOTTY

A fisherman and seafood dealer. He lives in a house-boat in Yarmouth. Brother of Clara Peggotty, he is a simple, good-natured man and totally unselfish.

## HAM PEGGOTTY

Orphaned nephew of Dan Peggotty, with whom he lives. Becomes a fisherman and boat builder, is engaged to Little Em'ly, and deserted by her, dies trying to save her seducer. A quiet, considerate, manly individual even though rough-hewn.

## LITTLE EM'LY

Orphaned niece of Dan Peggotty with whom she lives. Pretty, intelligent, affectionate, but beset with a desire to rise socially above her environment. This causes her to be seduced by Steerforth, who promises to make her a "lady." Later, deserted and remorseful, she emigrates to Australia with her uncle.

## MRS. GUMMIDGE

Widow of Dan Peggotty's former partner. She is the housekeeper at Yarmouth, a complaining, moody woman, who surprises everyone by her sudden strength of character in adversity. Goes to Australia with the Peggottys.

## MR. BARKIS

The Yarmouth carrier (combination taxi and truck driver). A taciturn man who woos and wins Peggotty with an almost wordless courtship. He dies leaving her well-off financially.

## MR. CHARLES MELL

Assistant master at Salem House School. He is underpaid, but cheerful (plays the flute). Dismissed after quarrel with his pupil, Steerforth. He turns up years later as Doctor Mell of Colonial Salem House School in Australia.

## TOMMY TRADDLES

Plodding but loyal school friend of David's at Salem House. Later helps David learn shorthand. He becomes a lawyer and assists in the unmasking of Uriah Heep.

## JAMES STEERFORTH

Handsome, lordly, egotistic school friend of David's at Salem House. Later he befriends David in London, tries to lead him in dissipation, and abuses his trust by seducing Em'ly. Self-centered, arrogant, inconsiderate, his weak character is the result of his mother's indulgence. Yet a charming person at first acquaintance.

## MR. CREAKLE

Ferocious headmaster at Salem House School. A former hop-dealer whose chief interest in education is in flogging the boys. Later turns up a magistrate running a "model" prison.

## MR. OMER

The Yarmouth undertaker-draper-tailor-etc. Fits David with mourning clothes for his mother's funeral. Later Em'ly works for him as seamstress.

## MR. JORAM

Helper, then son-in-law and partner to Mr. Omer.

## MEALY POTATOES AND MICK WALKER

Two boys who work beside David in the Murdstone and Grimby warehouse and whom he despises as "common."

## WILKINS MICAWBER

Happy-go-lucky, improvident, optimistic and a great talker and writer of flowery phrases. David lives with him in his warehouse days, and Micawber later becomes confidential clerk to Uriah Heep. After unmasking Heep, Micawber emigrates to Australia, where he becomes a magistrate. One of the greatest comic figures in English fiction.

## EMMA MICAWBER

Wife of Micawber. A loyal and devoted spouse who has an abiding faith in her husband's abilities. She shares his buoyancy and optimism while struggling against adversity and raising numerous children.

## RICHARD BABLEY, MR. DICK

A feeble-minded gentleman rescued from the lunatic asylum by the kindly Betsey Trotwood, with whom he thereafter lives. His directness of mind and genial simplicity often bring results where superior mental powers have failed.

## URIAH HEEP

Clerk in the law firm of Mr. Wickfield. Hypocritical product of a charity school, he hates the "upper" classes, and strives by cheating and plotting to make his way in the world. Gets Mr. Wickfield in his power and is forcing Agnes to marry him when he is exposed as a forger. Later turns up in Creakle's "model" prison, serving a life sentence.

## MR. WICKFIELD

Betsey Trotwood's solicitor (lawyer), in Canterbury. A widower, father of Agnes. His self-pity after his wife's death had led to drinking. Falls prey to machinations of Heep.

## AGNES WICKFIELD

David's second wife, the devoted daughter of Mr. Wickfield, Aunt Betsey's lawyer. An orphan, she, unlike Dora Spenlow, was not brought up in luxury, but at an early age took upon herself the running of the Wickfield home. Her father, proud of her precocious efficiency, calls her his "little housekeeper." She is sweet and placid, an aura of serenity and light is always described as surrounding her. David often remarks that "there is goodness, peace, and truth wherever Agnes is."

Agnes dutifully caters to her father, worriedly watches him slip drunkenly under the influence of the evil Uriah Heep, but never reproaches him. Although she loves David from the start, she shyly permits him to marry Dora without a hint of her own feelings. So self-effacing is she that she advises David in his romance with Dora, and even attends their wedding as a bridesmaid. Only David's fascination for the arrogant and sinister Steerforth calls forth a mild warning from her that he is David's bad angel.

The unassuming, ever-sweet Agnes hovers about in the wings during David's short-lived marriage. Dora, on her death-bed, realizing that Agnes loves David, turns him over to her. But years of separation still follow while David, rather dull-witted about Agnes, has to learn first that he loves her, and then that she loves him. As his wife she is his continuing inspiration and guide, the things he lacked in Dora. At the close of the book he sees her "face shining on him like a heavenly light."

## DOCTOR STRONG

Headmaster of Canterbury school where David is educated. Amiable, kind, but also untidy and absent-minded. Married to a woman much younger than he whom he loves even after suspecting her of infidelity. David later becomes his part-time secretary while learning shorthand.

## ANNIE STRONG

Beautiful young wife of Dr. Strong. She has a needy family that uses the marriage to exploit the doctor. Is faithful to her husband even though importuned by her former lover, Jack Maldon.

## MRS. MARKLEHAM

Known as the "Old Soldier." Mother of Annie Strong. A selfish, self-centered woman who uses her daughter's marriage to provide for her relatives. Tactless, she is responsible for the near-break-up of the Strongs' marriage.

## JACK MALDON

Annie Strong's cousin and former sweetheart. He is a ne'er-do-well sponger whom Mrs. Markleham provides for through Dr. Strong. He still has designs on Mrs. Strong, who repulses him.

## MRS. STEERFORTH

Widowed, imperious mother of James Steerforth. Her pampering and indulging of her son has made him an arrogant egotist. Her own love for him is selfish and possessive. When he elopes with Em'ly and alter drowns, she is devastated.

## ROSA DARTLE

Mrs. Steerforth's companion. A younger woman secretly in love with Steerforth, who toys with her affections. She is tempestuously moody, vindictive toward Em'ly.

## LITTIMER

Steerforth's valet and arranger of intrigues. When Steerforth tires of Em'ly he turns her over to Littimer to marry. Littimer always embarrasses the young David with his air of utter respectability. Turns up in Creakle's model prison.

## MISS MOWCHER

A dwarf hairdresser with social connections. At first is involved in Em'ly's seduction, but later is heroine responsible for Littimer's jailing.

## MARTHA ENDELL

Friend of Em'ly's who, seduced and abandoned, becomes a prostitute. Helps to find Em'ly, emigrates to Australia, and is rehabilitated.

## MR. FRANCIS SPENLOW

Proctor (lawyer) in Doctor's Commons to whose firm David is articled. Refuses David as future son-in-law, but dies insolvent soon after.

## MRS. CRUPP

Landlady of London boarding-house at which David lives which while a law apprentice.

## DORA SPENLOW

David's first wife, the daughter of his employer in Doctors' Commons. A girl brought up in sheltered luxury, she not only refuses to take harsh realities seriously, but does not even want to know about them. Pampered as a child, uneducated to practical concerns, she makes David a loving but inept "child-wife." Like a typical woman of her class, having been surrounded by servants, she knows nothing of housekeeping or domestic management. She has no desire to learn, nor is she capable of learning even if she has to. She is, of course, a hindrance to the struggling young author, and she conveniently dies after a few years of marriage to make way for Agnes.

A psychologist would say that David was attracted to her in the first place because she is so much like his own mother. Mrs. Copperfield, too, had been thought of as a "wax doll" wife, a loving but soft, pliable and weak-willed woman incapable of getting on except for the help of Peggotty and no match for the unscrupulous Mr. Murdstone.

## JULIA MILLS

Dora's girlhood confidante. A somewhat disillusioned romantic, she later goes to India and marries an elderly but wealthy merchant.

## SOPHY CREWLER

Long suffering, patient sweetheart of Tommy Traddles, one of ten daughters of a poor clergyman. Cheerful in poverty after marriage, she helps her husband in his career.

# DAVID COPPERFIELD

## CRITICAL COMMENTARY

· · · · · · · · · · · · · · · · · · · · · · · · · · · · · · · · · · · · · · · · · · · · · · · · · · · · · · · · · · · · ·

### EARLY RECEPTION

*David Copperfield* appeared in twenty monthly parts from May, 1849, to November, 1850. In the preface to a later hardbound edition of the book, Dickens wrote: "Of all my books, I like this the best" and "... like many fond parents, I have in my heart of hearts a favourite child. And his name is David Copperfield." The public, unfortunately, did not at first share this enthusiasm. While the monthly parts of the preceding novel. *Dombey and Son*, had sold 32,000 copies on an average, the sales of *David Copperfield* were only 25,000 copies each month.

One of the reasons for this falling off of readers is that *Copperfield,* unlike *Dombey,* is realistic rather than melodramatic, at least in its first parts. The term **realism** was not applied to fiction until 1855, when it was used by the critic G. H. Lewes, who did not consider the novels of Dickens realistic. Another contemporary critic felt that this real-life quality was due to the autobiographical element. This unknown critic hailed the novel in the *Prospective Review*, VII(1851), as "a signal triumph over the disadvantages of a bad form," meaning the serialized novel, which he considered "the lowest artistic form yet invented." The same critic continues by praising the author for having "succeeded in identifying himself with his principal personage. Every line is coloured with the hues of memory...."

It is this subjectivity, so important in modern, fiction, that has made *David Copperfield* the most popular of Dickens' novels in the twentieth century. Richard Aldington, writing in *Four English Portraits* (1948), points out that of the thousand or more titles in the *Everyman's Library* series, *David Copperfield* outsells all the rest year after year. There are more different editions of the novel in print today, both hardbound and paperback, than of any other Dickens work.

## MODERN VIEWS

Modern critics have substantiated the common reader's admiration. Edward Wagenknecht in his *Cavalcade of the English Novel* (1943) calls *David Copperfield* "the most beloved piece of fiction in the English language ...: fundamentally the book is God's truth." Walter Allen, while agreeing that the novel is realistic, "his one attempt at something that may be called realistic," feels that though it is marvelous, it is a failure.

Ernest A. Baker, in his monumental *History of the English Novel*, Volume 7 (1936), devotes nine pages to *David Copperfield*. He too, considers that "nowhere else ... does Dickens appear so true a realist." He points out that although there are some "melodramatic excrescences on what may be regarded as the authentic story" it does "read like the literal truth. The characters are as solid as the ground they stand on."

Baker asserts that people like Murdstone and Creakle are not caricatures, but men of flesh and blood, "only too faithfully reproduced." They are seen and described just as a small boy would. David's idolatry of Steerforth is also a boy's worship of one older and more sophisticated than himself. If takes him a long time to realize that his idol has feet of clay, but realization comes with maturity.

Baker denies that although Dickens conveys "his experiences with a vigour and incisiveness beyond all praise," he yet himself seems "to dissolve and fade out of the picture," as other critics have charged. "David Copperfield emerges a real man," he writes. "He is not literally Dickens the novelist."

## EDGAR JOHNSON

Edgar Johnson, whose biography promises to be the definitive one, also thinks that while *David Copperfield* does not literally portray the actual life of Dickens, it does mirror his emotional development. He finds deeply revealing the parts of his real past that Dickens uses, and those he either leaves out or changes. "Both the suppressions and the fantasy are profoundly indicative of the wounds that were still unhealed after a quarter of a century," he writes.

The Murdstones, for example, have no real counterparts in the childhood of Dickens. Yet in the pair Dickens is symbolically punishing his parents: his father for whose improvidence he was condemned to the blacking warehouse; his mother who wanted him to stay there even after the family fortunes had improved. While not at all like his real parents, they are symbols of "parental love ... turned into indifference and neglect." Actually Mr. and Mrs. Micawber are more like John and

Elizabeth Dickens. Mr. Micawber's financial irresponsibility and his pompous utterances are those of the elder Dickens. Mrs. Micawber's ineffectuality and careworn domesticity are those of Mrs. Dickens. And just as David loves Micawber for all his faults, so did Dickens love his father and constantly bail him out of debt.

Edgar Johnson considers that *David Copperfield* is the most successful portrayal of childhood in fiction. He writes that James Joyce in *A Portrait of the Artist as a Young Man* "paints the bewilderment and unhappiness of childhood, but not its delights and affections." Even *Tom Sawyer* and *Huckleberry Finn*, "superb though they are, do not have the scope nor even quite the depth of *David Copperfield*."

## ANDRE MAUROIS

Andre Maurois, the French writer and critic, in his study *Charles Dickens* (1935), claims that Dickens in his novels personifies the British optimistic philosophy. "Something is bound to turn up" is not only the philosophy of Mr. Micawber, but of Dickens and the whole British people, "Mr. Micawber," he writes, " is the ultimate symbol of the Dickensian man, and the first words of the Dickensian 'message' might run: 'Have confidence; be cheerful; the world belongs to those who set out to conquer it with a sure heart and a good humour.'" Maurois is among a number of critics who point out the fairy-tale quality of parts of *David Copperfield*. The ending of the novel is a fairy-tale ending: all the characters who have emigrated to Australia "are miraculously consoled for their griefs and cured of their faults." Edgar Johnson writes that Betsey Trotwood is "plainly as may be the fairy godmother of the nursery tales," who "with a single wave, as it were, of her wand, ... sends the Murdstones reeling backward, and the warehouse, that dark place of tears, disappears forever."

## BRUCE MCCULLOUGH

Bruce McCullough in *Representative English Novelists: Defoe to Conrad* (1946), devotes a chapter to *David Copperfield*. According to him, both the glory and weakness of Dickens is a result of a his close attention to the public response to his novels. "A devotee of the theater, he saw his novels as a series of stage effects. Issuing them in parts, he could watch their effect month by month and alter them to suit his readers without to their inner logic." he writes. This is true even of *David Copperfield*, which "proceeds by a series of surprises rather than by a natural process of development from within."

McCullough is close to Maurois in his estimate of the Dickens philosophy, but he finds it rooted in eighteenth-century primitivism. Thus the "good characters are instinctively good-natured and generous," while in the bad, "the natural affections have suffered atrophy or extinction." The code of this philosophy or way of life is expressed in Betsey Trotwood's plea to David: "Never be mean in anything; never be false; never be cruel."

This philosophy of loving kindness, according to McCullough, permeates the novel. Aunt Betsey through kindness helps the lunatic Mr. Dick lead a useful life. Mr. Peggotty and David by their trust and sympathy rescue Martha Endell from a life of prostitution. Loving kindness saves the marriage of Dr. Strong and his wife. Loving kindness, implies Dickens, will do more to solve the ills of society than will institutions or organized philanthropy. He was later to have his doubts about this, but in *David Copperfield* the feeling is still strong.

Finally, McCullough examines Dickens as a humorist, pointing out that he was at one time though of primarily as a comic writer. *David Copperfield* abounds in comic situations: the dinner which is eaten by the waiter, David's courtship of Miss Larkins, the Barkis-Peggotty wooing, Dora's dinner for Traddles (with the unopenable barrel of oysters). Micawber is obviously meant to be a comic character, but what of some of the others? Is the wooly-minded Mr. Dick supposed to be laughed at? Or the dwarf, Miss Mowcher? Or Traddles with his multitude of sisters-in-law? Even evil in *David Copperfield* is slightly ridiculous, "not something capable of destroying us," writes McCullough. Uriah Heep is a low-comedy ogre, and we never really fear him. McCullough states: "To turn everything into humor is a way of escaping bitter truth." The Victorian reader was not yet ready to swallow the truth without a sugar coating. Thus humor, along with sentiment and horror, is a chief ingredient of Dickens' novels, and all elements are blended into his distinctive formula.

Robert Morse, writing in the *Partisan Review* in 1949, noted: "It is harder to sum up Dickens in a phrase or two than almost any other writer except Shakespeare or Dante." The reason for this is that Dickens is everything to everyone; he has something for everybody. Charles Dickens looking down from the literary Valhalla doesn't care why people still read him, as long as do read him. And they do.

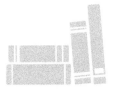

# DAVID COPPERFIELD

Question: To what extent is *David Copperfield* an autobiographical novel?

Answer: In its broad outlines the story of *David Copperfield* is that of the early life and career of Charles Dickens. That D. C. is but the initials of the author's name in reverse is not just a coincidence. The following are some of the correspondences:

A. David is taken out of Salem House School and out to work in the warehouse of Murdstone and Grinby in London.

   Dickens was taken out of Chatham School and out to work in the blacking warehouse of James Lamert in London.

B. Micawber, with whom David is living, is imprisoned in the King's Bench Prison for debt. His family soon moves in with him, and David visits them there.

John Dickens, Dickens' father, was imprisoned for debt in the Marshalsea Prison. His family moved in with him and Charles visited them there.

C.  David works as an articled clerk in the law firm of Spenlow and Jorkins in Doctors' Commons. Later he takes up shorthand and becomes a parliamentary reporter.

Dickens worked as an office boy for the law firm of Ellis and Blackmore in 1827. He also took up shorthand and became a parliamentary reporter in 1832.

D.  David begins writing "in a small way" and has his material published.

Dickens late in 1832 began writing sketches of London life and short stories which were published in the Monthly Magazine.

E.  After the success of his first work of fiction, David gives up reporting in order to devote himself full-time to writing.

After the success of *Pickwick* in 1837, Dickens gave up his reporting job on the *Morning Chronicle*.

Question: What elements of **satire** does *David Copperfield* contain?

Answer: *David Copperfield*, in contrast to most of Dickens' novel, contains relatively little **satire**. One satirical **episode** is the Waterbrook dinner party in Chapter 25, in which Dickens unlimbers his wit against the fatuous snobs prating about the "Blood," which is to them so all-important. Most of the guests are only middle-class social climbers who are "name-dropping" their aristocratic connections.

The chapters dealing with David's law career contain satirical comments on the law and lawyers, ever a favorite Dickens target. See especially Chapter 33.

The **episode** in Chapter 61, in which David inspects Creakle's "model" prison, seems to be brought in almost solely for the purpose of lambasting the wasteful expense of such institutions and their futility in effecting criminal reform. Prisons and criminals are another Dickensian near-obsession, touched on in nearly every novel.

Question: What does Dickens say in *David Copperfield* about education?

Answer: Dickens is expressing his ideas on education in contrasting the two schools David attends, Creakle's and Strong's. One is bad education, the other good, implies Dickens. Salem House School is run by a brutal ignoramus, a former hop-dealer turned "educator," probably because it was profitable and allowed him to indulge his sadistic lust for flogging children. The teachers were underpaid starvelings, the pupils badly housed and fed, and still worse taught. Education here consists of mechanical exercises done under the threat of severe flogging for errors or inability to learn.

At the Canterbury school taught by the scholarly Dr. Strong, things are different. The "honour and good faith" of the pupils is appealed to, not their fear. They felt, accordingly, that they "had a part in the management of the place" and behaved themselves like responsible individuals. They not only learned willingly, but had plenty of liberty, and all sorts of games.

Dickens corroborates his theory that love, not fear, should motivate learning by describing how well the little David had learned under his mother's affectionate tutoring, but how he proved a dunce under the harsh lesson plans of the Murdstones.

Question: What effect did serial publication have on the structure of *David Copperfield*?

Answer: From the viewpoint of novel structure, serialization makes *David Copperfield* a flawed novel. All one has to do is compare it to another novel which is an account of a boy growing into manhood, Henry Fielding's *Tom Jones*. *David Copperfield* lacks the unity of *Tom Jones*, the architectonic structure carefully built chapter by chapter to a satisfying climax.

A careful reader can determine where each of the monthly parts of *David Copperfield* ended. In each part there is a little **climax**, and then another story-thread is begun. In order to sustain interest, suspense is drawn upon constantly, and because the main story, David's life, cannot furnish enough, several subplots are introduced. Some, such as the Wickfield-Heep affair, affect David's life directly. Another, the Little Em'ly-Steerforth affair, affects him only because he feels responsible. Still another, the affair of the Strong's marriage, affects him only as a spectator. The effect of this is that in the latter half of the novel, David's life recedes into the background and we lose interest in him.

If we examine these subplots, we see that except for the first, they are poorly motivated. Why should a girl as well brought up as Em'ly succumb so easily to Steerforth, and without its being noticed? The conduct of Dr. Strong and his wife toward each other is not only inexplicable and absurd; it smacks of the pathological.

Finally, serialization demanded that each part repeat past **episodes** or information previously given in order to refresh the reader's memory. This contributed to the inordinate length of the novel.

Question: How did the relationship of Dickens with his parents perhaps affect the family backgrounds of the characters in *David Copperfield*?

Answer: When Dickens was taken out of school and put to work at the blacking factory, he felt that he had been deprived of parental love and protection, had been orphaned in a way. Orphaned or semi-orphaned children or adults play a very large part in his novels. Note the following cases in *David Copperfield*:

David Copperfield has no father, then no mother. Em'ly, Ham, Rosa Dartle and Traddles have no parents. Steerforth, Uriah Heep, and Charles Mell have no fathers. Agnes and Dora both have no mothers. In fact, the only complete family is that of the Micawbers. In spite of their precarious financial position, they enjoy togetherness of a genuine family life. This is the type of family Dickens liked to picture, and in the Cratchits of *A Christmas Carol* he gives us another example.

Question: How does *David Copperfield* rank as a "humorous" novel?

Answer: Among his contemporaries, Dickens enjoyed a great reputation as a humorist. He began his career with the *Pickwick Papers*, a novel (really a collection of episodes) in which humor is the chief ingredient. This humor is close to farce, a wild exaggeration, absurdity carried to its utmost. The best example of this type of humor in Pickwick is the account of the election at Eatanswill. In a later book, *Nicholas Nickleby*, an element of farce is the bit about the Hot Muffin and Crumpet Company. In each case, farce depends upon outrageously absurd situations, rather than people.

By *David Copperfield*, Dickens' humor had become more conscious and sophisticated. Farce of the earlier type still occurs, notably in the account of the waiter who eats David's dinner (Chapter 5), and in the Traddleses dinner given by the newly-wed David and Dora (Chapter 44). But most of the humor now is that growing out of personalities, rather than situations. Thus Mr. Micawber makes us laugh every time he appears: it is his reaction to situations that is incongruous and therefore funny, not the situations themselves. These are often tragic: unemployment, eviction, destitution, imprisonment.

Sometimes the humor is mixed with terror. Little David's strange encounter with the mad old-clothes dealer in Chatham after he has run away from the warehouse (Chapter 13) is one of these episodes. Little David is hungry and desperately in need of money, but is kept waiting all day while the drunken old madman tries to get him to accept all sorts of useless objects in exchange for the jacket David wants to sell. The affair strikes us as funny, but to David it must have been a terrifying experience.

In *David Copperfield*, Dickens uses humor to provide relief from the otherwise straightforward account of a boy's growing up in the world. His humor, like his melodrama, was a device to sugar-coat the otherwise bitter pill of social reform which he wanted his readers to swallow.

Question: What inferences about the personal philosophy of Dickens can be drawn from *David Copperfield*?

Answer: Because the novel is in so large part autobiographical, we can examine the views of David with some probability that they coincide with those of his creator, Charles Dickens. Especially revealing are the "golden rules" which David sets down at the beginning of Chapter 42:

"Even though this manuscript is intended for no eyes but mine," he writes, but Dickens means for us to know the dynamism of his personality. The source of his success is simply his "perseverance" and his "patient and continuous energy." He admits that he has neglected talents and wasted opportunities. "I do not hold one natural gift, I dare say, that I have not abused." But, he goes on, "whatever I have tried to do in life, I have devoted myself to do well; that whatever I have devoted myself to, I have devoted myself to completely; that in great aims and in small, I have always been thoroughly in earnest." Talent and opportunity may help men mount the ladder to success, he feels, but in the long run "there is no substitute for thorough-going, ardent, and sincere earnestness."

This gospel of sober industriousness, a heritage of the Protestant ethic that motivated the lower and middle classes since the days of Cromwell's Puritans, Dickens shared with most of his readers. Financial and social success are the rewards on earth for the faithful adherent to this doctrine, and Dickens' audience rejoiced with David Copperfield when his dreams came true.

Question: Describe some of the subplots in *David Copperfield*.

Answer: The main plot involves the childhood and later career of the hero. Skillfully woven into this are several subplots in which he is either directly involved or functions as a spectator. Besides providing a series of minor climaxes to add suspense to the monthly installments of the novel, the subplots with their many characters and situations also add color and texture to it.

The most striking of the subplots is that involving Little Em'ly and James Steerforth. The pretty daughter of the humble fisherman catches the eye of Steerforth, David's lordly and spoiled school-friend. Always dreaming of being a "lady," she succumbs to his blandishments, although she is engaged to her cousin, Ham. She runs away to the Continent with Steerforth on the eve of her wedding. He soon tires of her, especially since she becomes conscience-stricken, and he leaves her to be married off to his valet, Littimer. Remorseful, she escapes and makes her way to London, where she intends to lose herself in the lower depths of the metropolis. She is found by her uncle and taken with him to Australia, there to begin life anew. Steerforth, in the meantime, has been on a cruise, is ship-wrecked off the Yarmouth shore where he first met Em'ly, and is drowned. Also dying with him is Ham, who has tried to rescue him, not knowing who it was.

Another subplot is that involving the lawyer Wickfield (David's second father-in-law) and Uriah Heep, his scheming clerk. Heep, a hypocritical product of the charity school, always prates of being 'umble, but he secretly aspires to his employer's business and even his daughter, Agnes. He manages to work his way into a partnership by cleverly playing upon Mr. Wickfield's fondness for the bottle. Soon he runs the firm and embarks on a career of forgery and embezzlement, ruining Aunt Betsey financially. He is about to force Agnes into marrying him, when he is exposed by Mr. Micawber, who has become his confidential clerk. After a subsequent piece of criminal activity he is sentenced to prison.

The affairs of Mr. and Mrs. Micawber and their numerous offspring are another thread of subplot, besides providing a constant note of comedy. The impecunious Micawber is first met but a step removed from the debtor's prison. After many ups and downs, mostly the latter, we finally hear from him as a magistrate in Australia.

The strained marriage of the scholarly but elderly Dr. Strong and his young wife, Annie, is another subplot, but one in which David Copperfield functions as a mere spectator. The peculiar wooing of Peggotty by the taciturn Barkis, who is willin', and eventually wins her, provides a bit of love interest at the start of the novel; the long-drawn-out and rather comical romance of David's friend, Traddles, with his Sophy (one of ten daughters of a clergyman down in Devon, we are always being reminded), provides some at the end.

It is significant that all of these subplots in some way deal with love, of various types and degrees, good or destructive. Steerforth "loves" Em'ly as an object of pleasure, a toy to be abandoned when he grows tired. Heep "loves" Agnes Wickfield as a status symbol; she is the gentleman's daughter, his employer's, and in her he sees the apex of his ambitions for social climbing. Positive or good, in contrast, is the love of Barkis for Peggotty, or of Traddles for Sophy. The deep and abiding love that the Micawbers have for each other is the force that keeps them ever-optimistic and sees them through, even though Dickens treats it in a comic way. A careful study of the novel will reveal more of these relationships.

# FURTHER RESEARCH

## FURTHER ARTICLES ON DAVID COPPERFIELD

It is impossible to list the many articles that have appeared on *David Copperfield*. The student is referred to the following scholarly periodicals which contain some of this material:

*The Dickensian*, a quarterly published in London by the Dickens Fellowship.

*Nineteenth Century Fiction*

*Publications of the Modern Language Association* (PMLA)

*Victorian Newsletter*

*Victorian Studies*

## SUGGESTIONS FOR RESEARCH PAPER TOPICS

*David Copperfield* and Dickens' View of Childhood

Dickens' Real Childhood and *David Copperfield*

Growing up in early nineteenth-century England

London scenes in the early nineteenth century

Dickens' view of education as seen in *David Copperfield*

Dickens' view of lawyers as seen in *David Copperfield*

Dickens' view of prisons as seen in *David Copperfield*

Dickens and Class-snobbery

Dickens as champion of the common man in *David Copperfield*

Was Dickens himself a snob?

*David Copperfield* as a study of various types of love

*David Copperfield* as a study of various types of marriage

Dickens as a social reformer in *David Copperfield*

The Philosophy of Dickens as expressed in *David Copperfield*

The structure of *David Copperfield*

The use of symbols and **imagery** in *David Copperfield*

The effect of serial publication on David Copperfield

The reception of *David Copperfield* in its time

The critics and *David Copperfield*

Where does *David Copperfield* stand today?

Why read *David Copperfield*?

Lightning Source UK Ltd.
Milton Keynes UK
UKHW021248190721
387406UK00011B/2432